THE
CHRISTIAN
BOOK
OF THE
DEAD

THE
CHRISTIAN
BOOK
OF THE
DEAD

Angelo Stagnaro

A Crossroad Book
The Crossroad Publishing Company

Nihil Obstat: Reverend John P. Cush. S.T.L., Diocesan Censor
Imprimatur: Most Reverend Nicholas Di Marzio, Ph.D., D.D., Bishop of
Brooklyn
August 30, 2010

The Crossroad Publishing Company
www.CrossroadPublishing.com
©2010 by Angelo Stagnaro

All scripture quotations in this publication are from the Good News Trans-
lation in Today's English Version—Second Edition. Copyright ©1992 by
American Bible Society. Used by Permission.

Acquisition:	The Crossroad Publishing Company
Design:	Eve Vaterlaus
Development and editing:	John Jones, Sylke Jackson
Layout and Proofreading	Scribe Inc.
Cover design:	Wendy Bass

Library of Congress Cataloging-in-Publication Data is available from the
Library of Congress.

ISBN-13: 978-0-8245-2614-6 (paper)

TABLE OF CONTENTS

A Book for the Living — 1

What Can Death Do for You? — 8

How to Develop Healthy Spirituality — 15

Why Prayer Matters — 25

Like a Grain of Wheat — 35

The Power of Fasting — 41

We Are Not Perfect — 45

Paradise Begins Here on Earth — 50

All You Need Is Love — 57

Keeping Vigil with Our Dead — 67

Heaven or Hell? — 75

The Astounding Grace of Purgatory — 78

The Final Curtain — 84

Tasting Heaven — 91

Days We Are One Family — 97

The Wondrous Pilgrimage Toward Love — 109

Office of the Dead — 114

Notes — 125

A BOOK FOR THE LIVING

When I tell people I'm a stage magician, I often get a double-take. When I add that I'm also a Christian, people are even more intrigued, because the two don't seem to fit. People ask, "Aren't the two in conflict with one another?"

Not at all. What connects stage magic and illusions with legitimate religion is our dedication to and comfort with mystery. In fact, Christians refer to a teacher of *mystery*—that is, the person assigned to give instruction in prayer and the mysteries of the Faith—as a "mystagogue," because prayer is our entry point into Christian mystery. I'm a magician because I love the intersection of the hidden and the revealed. Coincidently, it's also the reason I'm a Christian. We both deal in mystery.

To be clear, I'm a magician, not a sorcerer. Sorcery, or "real magic," simply doesn't exist. If it did, people would hire witches, not mere magicians, to perform at parties. I've been a stage magician for over thirty years. I've traveled and lived in many countries of the world studying, performing, and teaching magic. Through this experience, I've learned that there are legitimate mysteries in life, and there are simple tricks. It's important to learn the difference.

The reason magicians don't tell their secrets is because they are simple and rather ridiculous. If you knew how the trick worked, you'd be disappointed. A mystagogue, on the other hand, is not trying to trick you; rather, he is presenting all Christian mysteries to anyone who earnestly wants to understand them. The reason we marvel at the stage magician's art is because we only see a partial picture, the part the performer wants us to see. In Christianity, however, we see, at least to the degree we are able, the whole glorious picture. Death and life really do form two parts of the great cosmos, the catholic ("universal") whole. This book pulls aside the curtain that supposedly separates them so that you can see the reality of life and death: the beautiful mystery of our Faith.

Death is the ultimate mystery in our lives. Westerners live highly sanitized lives by avoiding any reminder of death. Many of us go to great lengths to appear younger than our actual years. Or we avoid funerals and all talk of dying. In doing so, we become more frightened and apprehensive about death and dying. This is a great tragedy. As with magic, there's more to death than meets the eye. The principle illusion of death is that it is an end, a cessation of life and of everything we've done or loved. This is not simply true. There is life after death. Christianity offers an all-embracing vision for what death means and what it tells us about the meaning of our lives here and now.

✝

All children, teenagers, and young adults believe themselves to be indestructible and immortal. I recall how, at age twelve, three friends and I jumped out of a second-story window into an enormous pile of leaves we had pushed up against our house. We took no thought about our safety. My mother was furious. Once, I agreed to go kayaking in the Pacific Ocean, even though I didn't even know how to swim at the time. I recall the way I used to wander thoughtlessly into dangerous neighborhoods. Thinking back, I wonder how I survived my adolescence considering the great chances I took with my life. When we are young, death seems impossibly far away—life is so present to us that we are not likely to think much about what happens when we no longer draw breath.

As adults, however, all of us eventually come to grips with the fact that we are not immortal. You look at the tremendous physical suffering of the world and begin to ask what it all means. You witness a dear friend or family member struggle with illness, and the more he or she faces the prospect of death, the more you do as well. You begin to feel the fragility of life and wonder what, if anything, will remain of you when your life is over.

When you are ready to take the next step in reflecting on death, *The Christian Book of the Dead* can help you—it focuses not on dying, death, or the afterlife, but on the connection between life and death, especially the way you can live in preparation for death.

This book of the dead is a distinctively Christian one. To the Christian, death and Final Judgment are in the hands of God, and thus there are no magic spells to help your soul navigate the journey *postmortem*. The way you lead your life while alive, however, is completely within your purview and control. So this book is a prefunerary text, a guide for learning about the path you may walk in this life, prior to death.

I wrote *The Christian Book of the Dead* to remind Christians what those in our ancient tradition—Jesus, the apostles and scripture writers, theologians, great mystics and teachers—reveal about the ultimate mystery that defines us as mortals and as believers. In death, we see our hope and our salvation from the suffering of this world. It is the culmination, for good or for bad, of all of the things we've done in our lives.

Although in a sense Christianity is a religion like others, when it comes to death, Christianity stands in strong contrast to many other traditions. This was clear in the life and death of Jesus Christ. He brought the afterlife into this life through His preaching about the kingdom of God being near, and He brought this life into the afterlife through His resurrection. This difference was clear as well with the first disciples and St. Paul, who made Jesus's defeat of death the focus of the young Christian faith. The first people to hear their message regarded this kind of afterlife as unusual, even impossible, and although Christianity has been around for 2000 years, these same teachings on life and death continue to strike many today as impossible.

The Christian Book of the Dead, therefore, is structured differently from *The Tibetan Book of the Dead*. While the latter describes the step-by-step process by which a soul migrates *after* death, *The Christian Book of the Dead* concentrates on our earthly pilgrimage prior to death. The focus of this book is living a Christian life in anticipation of your death, of moving from faithlessness to faith, being grateful for God's grace, and forgiving your enemies. It is impossible to sustain this commitment without a life of prayer directed to the Source of Love. This book discusses the conversion of heart and the need for you to die to yourself, dedicate yourself to the Golden Rule, maintain a spirit of penitence, and develop a virtuous life.

This short work shouldn't be considered the sum of Christian knowledge about spirituality and the Last Things. In fact, such a book would be impossible to write. Although one might assume that there are libraries full of official teachings about death and the afterlife, the Church maintains great humility about the Last Things. The Catechism of the Catholic Church, for example, deals with Purgatory in just a few pages. I offer this little book as a devotional and as a manageable reference for contemplating the reality of death. I want to offer you a window into the distinctive way that a Christian views death, the way that death and life should be seen as conditioning each other, belonging always together in the grand plan for creation that God has given us. Along the way, I will try to point to places where, in my experience, misunderstandings are likely. The more we avoid separating death and life, the more we will be able to separate the illusion from the reality.

Ecclesiastes says, "Someone who is always thinking about happiness is a fool. A wise person thinks about death" (Eccl 7:4).

Death, the ultimate mystery for all people, can help us discover what we hold in common and can show us the way to live.

WHAT CAN DEATH DO FOR YOU?

Picture in your mind the illusion of sawing a lady in half. A magician puts a female assistant inside a box and saws it in half, the blade cutting deeper and deeper. People begin to shift uncomfortably in their seats. At that moment, life and death are suspended.

It's a great magic trick because of the intense feelings it causes in the audience. Of course, the assistant emerges from the box unharmed.

Now picture yourself in a different kind of box. There you are: lying in your coffin, dead. Around you are people you've known—people you haven't completely alienated over the years.

This time, it's real, not an illusion. Now what?

When you imagine being at your own funeral, you have to confront both the mystery of what comes next and, looking to the past, the fact that *it's too late*. Once you're at your own funeral, it's too late to repair your reputation or change the way you have treated others. So you would be wise to consider your death long before it catches up to you.

Dom Lorenzo Scupoli, a sixteenth-century Italian priest and mystic, wrote one of Christianity's most important spiritual treatises, *The Spiritual Combat*. This book reveals the great advantages to be had from meditating upon your death.

According to Dom Scupoli, the only way to overcome the innate selfishness we all possess is to rely upon God. By trusting in God and accepting your penances, trials, and tribulations, you can achieve spiritual enlightenment: that is, unity with God. Dom Scupoli describes several benefits that come from contemplating your death. Each will lead you to a fuller understanding of God's love and plan for the universe, for humanity, and for each person:

❧ Knowing that you will eventually die forces you to become wise and weigh alternatives more clearly. Things that seem like your "right" show themselves as less wise as you grow older and closer to death. As Scupoli wrote, "With nothing we came into this world, and with nothing shall we leave it." There is little use in becoming overly attached to anything of this world.

❧ Death is inevitable and serves to remind you that all of your acts are directed towards one final end. By keeping this in mind, you can shed your attachments to the petty considerations and disturbances life sends your way. Death reminds you of your true nature and what is truly important in life.

✣ When you consider the fact that you *will* die, it is sobering to think you have limited time upon this earth. You have a choice set before you: to spend your life doing good or ill. The contemplation of death can be an excellent protection against committing evil.

✣ Your eventual death should serve as a reminder that you will be judged by your Creator. Christ says that you'll be judged exactly in the way you have judged others during your life. This should lead you to forgive all those who mistreat you.

To Dom Scupoli's list, I would add a few other advantages to mediating upon death in general, or your own eventual death in particular:

1. Knowing that death is the ultimate equalizer, and that others face the same destiny, you can gain a greater sense of identity and sympathy with others.

2. Knowing that death can come at any time can prompt you to do good to others now

rather than later. When speaking with your loved ones, you won't hesitate to remind them of your love for them. Acknowledging your eventual death will create in you a more loving spirit.

3. Knowing your death will eventually come, you are motivated to accomplish greater things. Everyone would like to die leaving something of value for the generations who follow.

4. There are millions of people who die every day around the world, and yet the world moves forward. This should humbly remind us that no one is indispensible.

5. When you consider your death, you inevitably consider your life thus far and the great blessings you have been given. In counting your blessings, you realize the need to give as you've been given and are thus motivated to help others.

6. Realizing that you are incapable of totally controlling the circumstances of your life and your destiny can give you courage and a sense of divine providence, that portion or allotment God has planned for you.

In death we find life, and in life, death will inevitably come. In order to bring your mortality into your meditation, consider using the following questions:

🍂 *Imagine yourself on your death bed.* Who do you hope is with you?

🍂 What are they saying to you?

🍂 Are you ready to die?

🍂 What were your last wishes and final disposition of your possessions?

🍂 *Imagine yourself in your coffin.* Who has attended your wake and funeral?

🍂 What are they saying about you?

🍂 Who will remember and pray for you after you die?

🍂 Is there anything you would have hoped to do while alive but hadn't yet?

🍂 What kind of life would you have wanted to live?

✼ What would you say to Christ when you stand before Him in judgment?

✼ What do you believe He would say to you?

✼ What do you find yourself wishing you had done before your death?

✼ (Now awake and refresh yourself and remember, "Eternity begins here and now.")

Questions such as these can help you make remarkable progress in your spiritual life.

St. Francis of Assisi taught that death was not to be feared, but rather loved. In fact, he called her "Sister Death."

> Be praised, my Lord, through our Sister Bodily Death,
> from whose embrace no living person can escape.
> Woe to those who die in mortal sin!
> Happy those she finds doing your most holy will.
> The second death can do no harm to them.
> —"Canticle of the Sun," A.D. 1224

Reflecting on why death is our Sister can powerfully guide you through the journey of life and death.

Inspire my living every day, Lord. I know You will not abandon me. Sister Death comes to one and all, and I am no exception. Her arrival heartens me. It inspires me. It comforts me. Death defines the character of my life. Inspire me by her presence. Show me your love. Enlighten me through my acceptance of Sister Death's presence in my life.

HOW TO DEVELOP
HEALTHY SPIRITUALITY

Once I was on a train traveling through Germany. As many magicians do, I was performing magic and mentalism tricks for my fellow travelers. I had just finished the tricks when a very tall passenger, a guest worker from Africa, ran toward me yelling. He was telling the crowd I was not really doing magic in the sense of some otherworldly power—he yelled, "This man is a fake!" Whenever I perform, even if impromptu, I always make sure my audience knows up front that all magicians and mentalists are fakes—if we are good at what we do, we entertain, but no one in the world can literally turn two ropes into one or read another person's mind. So the man, who hadn't heard the beginning of my performance, was really just accusing me of having told the truth!

The man was right to be so animated at the sight of what he thought was sorcery. After all, around the world every day, thousands of people present themselves as sorcerers, healers, and seers when in fact they are not.

So too in the spiritual world. So many paths offering so many promises for liberation, wisdom, and transcendence. In a world that offers you so many different spiritual paths, which one should you take? Does it even matter which one you take? An *apophatic* (negative) perspective on spirituality is helpful here.

Dionysius and the Apophatic Way

The *apophatic* way focuses on how to remove inaccurate ideas about God from our minds. By reflecting on what God is not—God is not a body, God is not light—we can avoid detours to our path and come to a deeper understanding of what God is. Some forms of this apophatic way appear in scripture, such as when Paul writes about God as being inexpressible and unknowable. This way was most clearly developed in the work of pseudo-Dionysius, particularly in his classic work *On Mystical Theology*. This short masterpiece has inspired and challenged countless seekers through the centuries.

Before attempting to understand what Christian spirituality is, let us consider several things it is not. Each of these ideas is a tempting, but ultimately unsatisfying, detour in your spiritual growth, and as you grow in your faith, you, too, will learn how to yell, "This is a fake!"

Power over the Universe

If your spirituality involves developing an "inner power," you're practicing magic and not Christian spirituality. If you're hoping to float, bilocate, or move objects with your mind, you've lost your spiritual focus. Learning to love your enemies and strangers is more important than setting up a stage magic show. Otherwise, you call attention to yourself rather than to the needs of those who are suffering. In such a situation, where you refuse to give up "power," compassion is impossible.

A Tool for Changing God

Christian spirituality is also not a means for manipulating God; it is a chance to let God change you. Prayer in a theocentric life allows God to replace your heart of stone with one of flesh (Ez 11:19).

A Source of Pride

Christian spirituality has nothing to do with being prideful and self-congratulatory. If you believe yourself to be advanced, superior, or enlightened, you're only fooling yourself. Unless you are truly becoming a more humble person, you aren't actually practicing spirituality. A true spirituality will give you greater clarity about your moral and spiritual shortcomings.

Focused on the Self

Humility will inevitably translate into a compassion for everyone you meet. Your spirituality must motivate you to help others. Unless you are moved to perform acts of mercy, you have not reached a spirit of true humility. Your spirituality must develop within you a spirit of ever-expanding compassion.

Ego Building

Christian spirituality doesn't feed your ego. It destroys it, step by step. No one in the world would suggest that the great spiritual masters in human history, Christian or otherwise, have been narcissists. Think of Mother Teresa, Mother Cabrini, Dorothy Day, Peter Maurin, Abbé Pierre Grouès, St. Vincent de Paul, Pierre Toussant, Sœur Emmanuelle Cinquin, and so many more whom we meet in everyday life—all of them models of generosity and self-giving.

Fleeting

If your spirituality is on-again, off-again, all you've done is create a hobby or a way to pass the time rather than create a way of life. It is only a matter of time until you get bored and abandon it. A legitimate spirituality is life-sustaining and self-sustaining. It motivates you to accomplish even the impossible.

Only Feeling

Many things feel good, but not everything is good for you. A stoner's high, or for that matter a runner's high, is not the same thing as spiritual progress.

A Possession or Goal

No matter how attached you may be to your possessions, Christian spirituality isn't an accessory, an object you add to your life. Neither is it a goal to be achieved. If you are actively striving towards a spiritual experience, however you define it, you're destroying any prospect of ever attaining it.

Self-Destructive

When we practice bad habits like drug use, excessive drinking, promiscuity, lying, bragging, jealousy, spitefulness, and greed, we're far away from true spirituality. Unrecognized and unrepentant alcoholics, for example, can't develop a healthy spirituality. Christians refer to the Deadly Sins as *deadly* because they destroy the soul and any prospect of spirituality.

A Form of Counseling

Christian spirituality is not the same as psychological counseling. The aim is not to learn more about yourself. Self-awareness is important in its own way, but in authentic Christian spirituality, you come to understand that you are not the center of the universe.

Exoticism

Christian spirituality is the opposite of exoticism. Following trends or fads such as a new form of yoga will offer nothing of spiritual value, and the novelty will wear off; a genuine spirituality will last forever.

Relativistic

Spirituality is not compatible with a relativistic morality. This is especially true if you are quite forgiving of your own foibles and sins, but hold everyone else to account for even the slightest inconvenience they may have caused you.

In Competition with Religion

You don't get to pick and choose. For Christians, spirituality and religion are irrevocably tied together. Without a structured grounding, without figuratively binding yourself to a tried and true system, you are setting yourself up as your own spiritual master. No one is smart or good enough to be her own teacher. When you're entirely on your own, there's no one around who can tell you whether or not you've lost your mind, or your ideas are worthwhile, effective, or healthy. Being immune to criticism is a nice form of entertainment, but it isn't spirituality.

Something New

Avery Cardinal Dulles frequently said that he would be immediately suspicious if he came up with anything novel in terms of religion and spirituality. None of us are capable of coming up with anything new. The Book of Ecclesiastes states that there isn't anything new under the sun. And even if there were, the only reason you should seek something new would be if you had already mastered what was old, tried, and true, and that had already brought millions of people toward spiritual enlightenment. You and I aren't there yet, and it's a safe bet we never will be.

Just Like Drug Use

One of the most dangerous things I hear from people ignorant of Christian spirituality is that a religious experience is indistinguishable from a chemically induced high. This is absurd. Anyone who has ever used drugs can tell you what happens after you get high—you crash and fall into depression and withdrawal. After abusing drugs for even a short time, you start to need more and more to achieve the same buzz. Drugs are a foreign chemical introduced into your body, and drug use has detrimental effects upon the body and mind. Legitimate religious experience, on the other hand, leaves you joyous, content, and motivated to perform great acts of generosity and mercy. As Teilhard de Chardin said, "Joy is the infallible sign of God's presence." One who lives a spiritual life will sin less; and when he inevitably sins, he will immediately seek to redress those mistakes. Finally, no one has ever died as a result of a mystical experience, and there has never been a mystic who held up a liquor store in order to get another chance to meet God in prayer.

An Act of Self-Interest

The natural end of spirituality is a life defined by compassion. Compassion is not the equivalent of enlightened self-interest any more than *Schadenfreude*, deriving joy from the misfortunes of others, is the equivalent of legitimate joy. Compassion cannot limit itself. Love can't be traded tit-for-tat. William Shakespeare reminds us of this in Portia's words to Shylock:

> The quality of mercy is not strain'd,
> It droppeth as the gentle rain from Heaven
> Upon the place beneath: it is twice blest;
> It blesseth him that gives and him that takes
> —*The Merchant of Venice*, act 5, scene 1

On this path you will discover, again and again, how moving closer to God also means moving closer to others.

True *spirituality* has to do with the spirit, just as materialism has to do with the material world— things we can see and touch. By keeping this in mind, we learn to distinguish between acceptable and unacceptable paths, the healthy and the unhealthy. The sole goal of developing a spirituality is to rediscover your humanity, to regain your innocence: that is, to find Eden once again, that state of existence where humans met and conversed openly, freely, and lovingly with their God. Being with God in this way is as close to being in Heaven as you can be on this side of the grave.

Don't abandon me, Lord. Retool me. Reshape me.
Show me the True Image in which you made me.

WHY PRAYER MATTERS

Christian prayer is one of the most difficult topics for many people to grasp. This is unfortunate since in fact nothing is more natural than to pray to the God who created you. The nature of prayer, however, has been obscured by many other forms of spirituality, as well as by mistakes that Christians themselves make.

As a magician, it's easy for me to see these mistakes. Magic involves the illusion that if a man or woman says the right words or waves a wand in the right way, something unusual will happen— often, something remarkable and wonderful. Magic relies on the wish all of us have that gaining our wishes could be so simple. Sometimes, unfortunately, we turn to prayer for that same reason—by saying the right words in the right way, God will automatically be compelled to grant something we ordinarily would never have gotten. Christian prayer, however, is radically different. Prayer is a way to develop a relationship with God. God's will is not changed through our prayers. We, however, are changed. We learn to quiet our own intentions and listen more closely to what God wants for our lives.

☩

There are many arguments why God can't exist, and each one can be refuted using sound logic. Yet logic itself is not the aim of the spiritual path. Christians seek a relationship with the living God. Why do Christians believe that God exists? What hope do we have that there is Someone looking out for the destiny of our souls? One of the most beautiful explanations is found in 1 Kings 19:11–12.

> "Go out and stand before me on top of the mountain," the Lord said to [Elijah.] Then the Lord passed by and sent a furious wind that split the hills and shattered the rocks—but the Lord was not in the wind. The wind stopped blowing and then there was an earthquake— but the Lord was not in the earthquake. After the earthquake there was a fire—but the Lord was not in the fire. And after the fire there was the soft whisper of a voice.

God speaks to us in the quietness of our hearts. To know Who He is, all you need do is stop talking and allow Him to speak to you. A Christian doesn't look for hill-splitting and rock-shattering hurricane winds, violent earthquakes, and great conflagrations. Any Christian who has felt God's presence in his life knows that God exists in the silence of his heart.

In other words, in order to encounter God, all you need to do is follow a bit of Jewish advice from Psalm 46:10:

הרפו ועדו כי־אנכי אלהים ארום בגוים ארום בארץ:
(Be still and know that I am God.)

Augustine and the God Within

Augustine of Hippo died in the early fifth century. One of the greatest intellects of his era, this influential bishop was one of the first Western authors to write a spiritual autobiography. His *Confessions* documents the path of his soul and mind as he considers, then ultimately rejects, a number of non-Christian paths in favor of Christian faith. Alongside the book's intellectual riches, we also find great wisdom for the heart. One piece of wisdom has inspired seekers for centuries. Speaking directly to God, he writes, *Interior intimo meo* (Dear God, you are closer to me than I am to myself).

The path toward God will never lead you away from your true self—God is even more a part of you than anything you usually think of as *you*.

Mystagogy—Initiation into the Mysteries

God watched over me before I knew Him and before
I learned sense or even distinguished between good
and evil, and He protected me and consoled me as a
father would his son.

—St. Patrick, *The Confession of St. Patrick*

Serious Christian theology is not for the faint of heart or mind. We have a virgin giving birth to a God/man who rose from the dead three days after He died, thus revealing that God was three Persons Who are one God. And much of this can't be proved physically, only metaphysically. This is why we rely upon *mystagogy* rather than physics to explain ourselves. This word is derived from the ancient Greek *mystes,* which refers to "an initiated person," and *agogos,* which means "guide" or "leader." Mystagogy is the initiation into religious mysteries and their accompanying practices. The instructor of mysteries is called a mystagogue. The subject is so important to Catholic Christians that there is a separate period of instruction in prayer, almost as lengthy as the period of the catechetical instruction, as part of a person's conversion to the Church.

Prayer is the way we come to understand the mystery that is Christ. We can pray as a community, as in the case of the Mass, or as individuals.

We can pray aloud, mentally in the privacy of our minds, or silently in the depths of our hearts. We are called to it by the Holy Spirit while simultaneously motivated to do so by the deep, unquenchable hunger in our souls. He created the emptiness in us so that we would seek Him out to fulfill us. We empty ourselves of the falseness that we have created that gives us the illusion of being complete, so that God can heal us. In prayer, we harbor no distractions or preconceptions. We shed our anxieties, sinfulness, and self-obsession and allow God to teach us to become the humans we were meant to be.

Preparing for Prayer

When considering a life filled with prayer, you should ask yourself some important questions:

- ✄ Do you pray?

- ✄ Why or why not?

- ✄ What do you think prayer is?

- ✄ How do you pray?

- ✄ When do you pray, and how often?

- Do you find it is important? Why or why not?

- Would you like to develop your prayer life?

- What were your experiences during prayer?

- How do you describe your connectedness with the world?

- What about your connectedness with others?

- Your connectedness with God Himself?

- Do you feel you would use prayer in your own life?

- How do you think prayer will affect your life?

Answering these questions will help prepare you to respond to God. In fact, the answers to these questions are the essence of prayer. Prayer is giving. Prayer is entering a loving relationship with the soul's Lover.

The simplest way to define prayer is as our response to God's presence in our lives, and our response to His invitation to meet Him. Christians who seek out God do so specifically in order to develop a relationship with their Creator. Like any relationship, it needs to be nurtured and developed. You speak, you listen, you learn, you love. You have to not give up and not be demanding; neither one is in keeping with the proper relationship between a child of God and God Himself. Those who love each other don't demand, they don't keep secrets, and they don't try to manipulate each other. And, most importantly, those who are in love share that love with others. It would be inconceivable to claim to be compassionate while remaining unforgiving or ungenerous with others. A virtuous life is the best gauge for knowing if your spirituality is functioning properly or not.

Prayer in the Christian context is the giving of oneself over to God. As there are several stages of growth in prayer, the Christian gives as he is capable. Using whatever vocabulary he has, he asks God for greater unity with Him. At its most basic stages, merely asking God for things that are needed during the day is acceptable as they show the proper relationship between creature and

Creator. It's important to bring our needs to God even though He already knows what we need (Mt 6:8). By telling Him what we think we need, we aren't planning on "securing the goods." Instead, we are growing deeper in our relationship with Him merely by spending time with Him in prayer. As this relationship develops we come to understand His wisdom in giving us not what we want but instead, what we need.

Prayer as a Way of Life

Prayer is not an on-again/off-again activity; it is a way of life. It must be engaged in often, with regularity and with fervor. Not having sufficient free time is not a valid excuse. In fact, it's when you are most pressured in life that you absolutely have to set aside time for prayer. Even if you are safe, happy, and satisfied, it's important to maintain profound gratefulness to God, being thankful that everything seems to be going your way, and remaining mindful of those who aren't as fortunate. In prayer, actively and attentively listen to God. Hear Him speak to you in the glories of nature, in the smile of an elderly neighbor, or in the empty outstretched hand of a stranger begging in the streets. You may also encounter Him when you are silent and quell your intellect. And in this silence of your soul, stripped of your ego, you find

Him in the center of your soul. To do so, you have to give up your preoccupation with yourself and see your proper place in the universe. The Psalm teaches this exactly:

> Lord, You have examined me and You know me. You know everything I do; from far away You understand all my thoughts. You see me, whether I am working or resting; You know all my actions. Even before I speak, You already know what I will say. You are all around me on every side; You protect me with Your power. Your knowledge of me is too deep; it is beyond my understanding. Where could I go to escape from You? Where could I get away from Your presence? If I went up to Heaven, you would be there; if I lay down in the world of the dead, You would be there. If I flew away beyond the east or lived in the farthest place in the west, You would be there to lead me, You would be there to help me. (Ps 139:1–12)

Being Christian means seeking out the God Who created you. Through prayer, you grow in faith and in your relationship with God, and this relationship will become manifested in your life in a variety of different ways, all for the benefit of others. The ego and self-love are the sole reasons for evil in our hearts and in this world. No one is without sin. An acknowledgment of this sinfulness is an important step on the path of reunification with Christ. This is why, as we will see, you must learn to die to yourself.

> *Lover of my soul. You called me out of darkness into the existence of this world. Your word is life. Bring me closer still to You by showing me Your love. Show me Your beauty. Let me lose myself in Your love.*

LIKE A GRAIN OF WHEAT

St. Augustine of Hippo keenly observed how fortunate it is that infants and small children have weak limbs—otherwise their selfishness would lead them to tear others apart. We adults, however, have strong limbs and are quite good at causing damage to others if we think they stand between us and what we want. *Dying to ourselves* is a way to train and control the unruly child we perpetually carry within us.

Christ uses a parable to explain this point. To follow him on the path of life, we must learn this art of dying to ourselves.

> I am telling you the truth: a grain of wheat remains no more than a single grain unless it is dropped into the ground and dies. If it does die, then it produces many grains. Those who love their own life will lose it; those who hate their own life in this world will keep it for life eternal. Whoever wants to serve Me must follow Me, so that My servant will be with Me where I am. And My Father will honor anyone who serves Me. (Jn 12:24–26)

The *grain of wheat* is your will or pride. Unless it is controlled, transformed, and shed, your soul can never attain a perspective centered on others. Without that, in turn, even the most basic ethics is impossible. There is no need for any rule of moral conduct if it is not founded on a deep respect for humanity in general. For such respect to exist, you need to humble yourself and love unconditionally. Otherwise, you will find yourself opportunistically looking for some unfair advantage over others, a way to profit. Christ's central message is one of love, but love can't sustain you if you try to use it for selfishly purposes. The seed that dies for the sake of others is reborn into a beautiful plant. Sacrificial love, the love that gives of itself, allows you to strip yourself of your self-love. This sacrificial love gives life.

Recognizing your pain and the pain of others is the first step towards dying to yourself. Through this dying, those who sleep can awake (Rom 13:11). No one says, "I have so much pleasure in my life; now I understand the pain others feel." Pleasure leads only to the desire for more pleasure; pain leads to love. As St. Theodore of Studios (A.D. 759–826) taught:

> How splendid the cross of Christ! It brings life, not
> death; light, not darkness; Paradise, not its loss. It is
> the wood on which the Lord, like a great warrior, was

wounded in hands and feet and side, but healed thereby our wounds. A tree has destroyed us, a tree now brought us life.

We die to ourselves when we acknowledge that others are our "other selves." We express this connection and love for our brothers and sisters who are near and far and separated by time—either those in the distant past or in the far future. Christians preach universal brotherhood and strive towards that ideal.

To die to yourself and thus allow others to live more fully, consider these small ways.

Prayer

A Christian who uses excuses not to pray is like a man who hits himself in the head with a hammer and then wonders why he has a headache. Prayer serves many practical and indispensible purposes. With it, you can dramatically change the kind of person you are. You can learn about the Love Which called us into existence. Prayer offers answers to the most important questions in life. And it's free.

The Corporal Works of Mercy

Corporal works of mercy serve physical needs. The first six are listed in Matthew 25:31–46, while the last comes from the Book of Tobit (4:3).

❧ Feed the hungry.

❧ Give drink to the thirsty.

❧ Clothe the naked.

❧ Shelter the homeless/ Offer hospitality.

❧ Visit the sick.

❧ Ransom captives/ Visit the imprisoned.

❧ Bury the dead.

The Spiritual Works of Mercy

The spiritual works of mercy provide for the needs of the spirit.

❧ Instruct the ignorant.

❧ Counsel the doubtful.

✄ Admonish the sinner.

✄ Bear wrongs patiently.

✄ Forgive offenses willingly.

✄ Comfort the afflicted.

✄ Pray for the living and the dead.

Simple Living

By living simply, you keep your life unclut-
tered, centered on God, and unattached to unim-
portant things.

*Awareness of the Political, Social,
and Spiritual Conditions of the World*

In Charles Dickens's *A Christmas Carol*, the
Ghost of Christmas Past tells Scrooge that the two
greatest enemies to mankind are Want and Ignorance. It is unconscionable for a Christian to live in
the world in intentional ignorance and conscious
stupidity. Caring for those who can't care for themselves is only possible when you are aware of their
suffering.

☩

Each of these simple acts kills the ego, step by step. With each step, the emptiness inside you is filled by God. You build a civilization of love by caring for others, and you care for others not because there's something in it for you, but because you truly see the face of God in your brothers and sisters.

We will now look at ways in which to shed our pride, and anything else that separates us from God's presence. God's grace is ever before us. We exist solely by the grace of God, but we must reach out to accept that which God offers. We knock and He answers. Fasting, abstinence, and prayer all help to strip us of our ego and progress upon the Christian path.

> With each step I take toward You, the Lover Who calls me out of darkness and chaos, I see You more clearly. I see You in the hearts and faces of those around me. I see You in the poor, the displaced, the homeless, the infirm, the lonely and hated, the wounded and the broken. I love You more and more each day. My heart trembles for You.

THE POWER OF FASTING

Any time you go to your neighborhood book-store or supermarket, you can see a variety of books about dieting, "detoxing," and other food-related forms of self-help. Fasting, a venerable tradition long fallen out of favor, has been making a comeback in recent years, and more books on it are appearing. But many people still misunderstand the *Christian* view of fasting.

Throughout history, and even today, many groups have encouraged fasting as a way to enter into a trance or gain magical powers. This is not the Christian way. Christians fast in order to "lose" power, that is, to let go of ourselves and give ourselves more fully to God.

Secondly, a Christian fast is not a diet, nor does it mean restricting the amount and kinds of food you eat merely to cleanse your body. It is meant in part to heighten awareness of the Holy and of the existence of suffering in the world. Traditionally, fasting referred to abstaining from or limiting food or drink at least for limited periods of time. Abstinence can also apply other behaviors. It is not as unusual as non-Christians might think. Alcoholics abstain from alcohol. Athletes are advised to abstain from smoking to improve their performance, and those who are true to their marriage vows abstain from sex with people other than their spouses. Even in the twenty-first century, fast-food restaurants report that, because of Catholics abstaining from meat, Fridays remain the biggest day for selling fish filet sandwiches.

Catholic Christians are required to fast on Ash Wednesday and Good Friday. This means that those between the ages of 18 to 59 who are able are requested to consume only one full meal with two smaller meals that cannot equal the amount in the full meal. This, of course, means that we abstain from meat on both of these days. Catholic Christians are required to abstain from meat on Ash Wednesday, Good Friday, and all the Fridays of Lent.

Fasting means refraining from food, or at least restricting the amount of food consumed, specifically for the purpose of developing one's spirituality. Abstention is the avoidance of certain foods or activities for the same purpose.[1] As most people know, it is customary to treat all of Lent as a period of fasting and penance by giving up a certain food or some other comforting item or activity, such as smoking, alcohol, bread, or dessert.[2]

☩

Like so many of the customs of our faith, Christians took the idea of fasting and abstinence from the Jewish tradition, where it was used in many of their religious rituals (1 Kgs 21:9; Ps 69:10; Isa 58:4; Jer 36:6; Dan 9:3). Fasting is not meant to punish anyone. Fasting and abstinence should bring joy into one's life. If it doesn't, you're doing it wrong! As Christ recommends:

> And when you fast, do not put on a sad face as the hypocrites do. They neglect their appearance so that everyone will see that they are fasting. I assure you, they have already been paid in full. When you go without food, wash your face and comb your hair, so that others cannot know that you are fasting—only your Father, who is unseen, will know. And your Father, who sees what you do in private, will reward you. (Mt 6:16–18)

As good as fasting is for us, however, it is like other good works. It won't get us into Heaven; grace alone brings us there. It is a sign of the joy we share as Children of God—it is an "effect" and not a cause of our being Christians.

Fr. Jim Van Vurst, OFM had some interesting ideas for alternatives to the Lenten traditional fasting. He suggested that we could give up:[3]

✖ insisting we are always right in any argument;

✖ controlling family members and others by means of anger or deadly silence;

✖ relying on a clever but sarcastic tongue that we might think is cute but hurtfully cuts others, even loved ones;

✖ wasting hours on the Internet when we could be doing something with our family.

There are other examples, of course, but you may find that the above suggestions are much more challenging than cutting down on food. Whatever practice you choose, however, fasting and abstinence are a necessary part of Christian spirituality. They counteract self-indulgence, which disrupts our journey on the path to spiritual maturity. Fasting is our gift to God. What else do you give to the God Who has *literally* everything? Fasting shows our repentance, our dedication, and our love. Penitence, we will see, offers similar benefits.

> *Lord, teach me the ways of the desert. I must*
> *increase as You decrease. Give me a heart*
> *of flesh to replace my heart of stone.*

WE ARE NOT PERFECT

I have been all things unholy. If God can work
through me, He can work through anyone.

—St. Francis of Assisi

If we say that we have no sin, we deceive ourselves,
and there is no truth in us. But if we confess our sins
to God, He will keep His promise and do what is right:
He will forgive us our sins and purify us from all our
wrongdoing.

—1 John 1:8–10

Recently, I was visiting an Italian monastery
when a monk entered the refectory for dinner. "I
just returned from the chapel," he said, "where a
woman told me she wanted to offer her confession. I encouraged her to do so prayerfully, but
she simply stopped and stared at me. Fearing that
something was weighing heavily on her heart, I
asked her what was wrong. She answered, 'Well,
I still think it's important to go to confession, but
I don't know what to say.' 'Remember any sins
you have committed,' I said, 'and humbly bring
them before God. The God we worship promises
that He will forgive a contrite heart.' 'But I haven't
committed any sins,' she replied." The monk was

shocked. "'In that case,' I said, 'please step out of the confessional so that I may kneel before and worship you.'"

The monk went on to explain to her that everyone sins, even himself, and perhaps she needed a little time to consider her interactions with others and with God.

☩

Today's popular culture suggests that we have the right to behave as we wish—or, if we admit that we are doing something wrong, we have several reasons for explaining away our bad behavior as something we were forced to do. Although this can seem like a form of compassion, trying not to be unforgiving of ourselves, this is really a form of self-worship, a symptom of the cult of the individual.

Gregory of Nyssa and the River of Time

Gregory of Nyssa was an early church leader, theologian, and preacher who had a major influence on our understanding of the Trinity. Like many in his day, he emphasized how important it was for our souls to cling to the unchanging nature of God rather than our own changing world. His poetic words can inspire us still today.

Let us therefore consider our transitory life and the passing, unstable nature of time, which, like a teeming river, carries everything away to destruction. Would that this brief, perishable life might be without guilt! Because we are subject to peril at each hour, we must be responsible to the incorruptible [i.e., unchanging] Judge. . . . Consider the constitution of the good soul and its royal dignity. Closely reflect upon the King of Kings and Judge of Judges and seek to live and behave well in accord with the commandments. In this way we may all attain the unblemished existence of [the Heavenly] city.[1]

Small Steps

Unfortunately, blind hubris and narcissism are not uncommon among us. Whenever we set ourselves apart from others and try to exempt ourselves from the standards we hold others to, we only feed our own anger and resentment. The only hope we have is what Christians call penitence— true sorrow for what we have done and a resolution to continue on the path of Christian virtue by relying on God's grace. Shedding our egos is the only way to live authentically as a loving child of a loving God. This is what is meant by dying to oneself.

Consider the following steps to practicing penitence in your life.

⚘ Your very existence is proof of God's omnipotence and omnibenevolence. Practice trusting it.

⚘ When you suffer, or even when you are inconvenienced a little, accept that pain and offer it up to God. Be like the Samaritan woman in the Scriptures, and ask God for the "waters of life" that He promised.

⚘ Form your prayers around your sorrow for having sinned.

⚘ Ask God for His forgiveness in your prayers.

⚘ Remain confident that God will forgive you.

⚘ Remember God's great mercy and ask Him for it.

⚘ Resolve to repent and change your behavior.

⚘ Ask God for the strength and wisdom to change.

⚘ Beg God to help you continue recognizing your own faults.

🦋 Allow God's forgiveness of you to translate into love and forgiveness of others who share your faults.

🦋 Set aside half an hour a day to spend reading Scriptures or spiritual treatises, in addition to time reserved for prayer.

🦋 In your daily life, remember not to be arrogant. We are all sinners, equally in God's eyes.

As we've seen throughout this journey, you can't hope to steer clear of detours, including the detours of sin, if you can't learn to recognize them. Consider the following prayer for deepening your awareness of sin and your willingness to ask for God's mercy.

> *Lover Who called me into existence. Without You, I am nothing. Without You, I can accomplish nothing. I am sorry for what I have done and what I have failed to do. I am sorry for my pridefulness, my hatred, my unkindness, my lack of generosity. I resolve this day, this hour, this moment to dedicate myself to You and Your will. Teach me to be kind, generous, gentle, and humble. In the Name of Your Son, Jesus Christ, I ask this of You.*

PARADISE BEGINS
HERE ON EARTH

A confessor I had as a young man once told me this story, which I later learned has been told in many forms.

A Benedictine monk was meditating in the woods, when along came a knight on horseback. This knight was known as a brawler, a drunk, and a bully. Seeing a praying monk as an easy target, he thought he would have some sport with him.

He jumped to the ground and walked over to the monk and pushed him.

"Monk! Teach me the difference between Heaven and Hell," he bellowed.

The monk never opened his eyes. Instead, he remained silent, not interrupting his prayer.

The knight, unaccustomed to having anyone defy him, was furious. He pushed the holy man again.

"Monk! Teach me the difference between Heaven and Hell," he roared.

Go away!" the monk replied. "You're rude, drunk, and obnoxious, and no one can stand being in your presence. And I might add, you smell worse than your horse."

At that, the knight became incensed. Blood suffused his face, and he intended on ending the insolent monk's life instantly. He drew his sword and raised it high above his head in order to cleave the hapless monk neatly in two for his remarks.

The holy man, without opening his eyes, spoke once again.

"And that is Hell."

The knight, taken aback by the words this defenseless monk spoke, stood in shocked silence. At that very movement, a flood of memories overtook the knight. Every lie, every theft, every instance of violence bombarded him. The pain he inflicted on others and upon his own soul crushed him. He fell to his knees and wailed aloud in the forest as tears ran copiously down his cheeks. He choked on the self-loathing and the sorrow he felt for all he had hurt.

The monk, without opening his eyes, spoke once again.

"And that is Heaven."

The moral of the story is clear: Heaven and Hell begin for us while we are here on Earth. Both are free choices, and only the interminably foolish or irrevocably evil would choose the later. Whatever we choose reverberates infinitely and throughout eternity. As Cicero taught us, *Aeternitas resonat vitae tamquam imago* ("Eternity is the very echo of our life"; *Tusculan Disputations* [book 3, chap. 2. 18]).

Attaining Heaven

Here and throughout our journey, we use language of space and time. We speak of the soul's "movement," about attaining Heaven, progressing on a path, and so forth. This language should not be understood too literally. Most theologians understand the biblical language of ascent and descent as metaphorical— we don't actually move up, down, or laterally. Hell, Purgatory, and Heaven are not somewhere else; they are a different kind of existence altogether and might equally well be called states rather than locations. Still, scripture writers and mystics throughout the years have taught us that this language is the best language we have for thinking about our distance from God and our yearning to draw closer to Him.

There is no magic spell for Christians to attain Heaven. No esoteric rituals. No eldritch secrets. The way to Heaven is and has always been to align your heart, mind, and soul with God. This is done through compassion and humility. As such perfected characteristics are impossible to attain on our own, you must rely upon God's grace to assist you. As St. Thérèse of Lisieux wrote in her *Story of a Soul*, "I wish I hadn't ever performed even a single act of charity in my life, so that when I stand before God's Throne, I might throw myself completely upon His mercy."

We can often be tempted to keep God on the peripheral on our consciousness rather than giving our lives completely. This is an invitation to great spiritual harm. Abba Joseph of Panephysis, one of the Desert Fathers, offers a wise story for the earnest Christian seeking to develop his or her spirituality:

> Abba Lot went to see Abba Joseph and said to him, "Abba, as far as I can I say my little office, I fast a little, I pray and meditate, I live in peace and as far as I can, I purify my thoughts. What else can I do?" Then the old man stood up and stretched his hands towards Heaven. His fingers became like ten lamps of fire and he said to him, "If you will, you can become all fl ame."[2]

These two stories shouldn't surprise any Christian. Christ specifically tells us what to do to attain His Father's Kingdom:

> Once a man came to Jesus. "Teacher," he asked, "what good thing must I do to receive eternal life?" "Why do you ask Me concerning what is good?" answered Jesus. "There is only One Who is good. Keep the commandments if you want to enter life." "What commandments?" he asked. Jesus answered, "Do not commit

murder; do not commit adultery; do not steal; do not accuse anyone falsely; respect your father and your mother; and love your neighbor as you love yourself." "I have obeyed all these commandments," the young man replied. "What else do I need to do?" Jesus said to him, "If you want to be perfect, go and sell all you have and give the money to the poor, and you will have riches in Heaven; then come and follow Me." When the young man heard this, he went away sad, because he was very rich.

Jesus then said to His disciples, "I assure you: it will be very hard for rich people to enter the Kingdom of Heaven. I repeat: it is much harder for a rich person to enter the Kingdom of God than for a camel to go through the eye of a needle." When the disciples heard this, they were completely amazed. (Mt 19:16–30)

This is the "formula" our Lord has given us for attaining Heaven. It's hard to try putting a different spin on such specific words. A Christian couldn't hope for a clearer map for how to get to Heaven. And yet, too many people who call themselves Christian willfully ignore these instructions. Many Christians could recite this passage from memory, so the problem isn't that people have forgotten it. It is just exceedingly hard advice for most Christians—for most anyone—to take. To attain Heaven, you must recognize yourself in the evil, selfish knight described previously. "The only solution," as Dorothy Day would say, "is love." By recognizing God's love, you can destroy the jail in which you've imprisoned yourself. In order to attain Heaven, you must, as St. Thérèse of Lisieux taught, call God your Father and know yourself as His child. By keeping your eyes upon God you come to understand your true nature and true goal in life (Phil 3:12–14). The world and everything in it that people desire is passing away; but those who do the will of God live forever (1 John 2:17). The Gospel of Matthew poignantly explains this. "Not everyone who calls Me 'Lord, Lord' will enter the Kingdom of Heaven, but only those who do what My Father in Heaven wants them to do" (Mt 7:21). By embracing death, we accept true, eternal life.

In the end, actions matter, and the chief rule in determining what is right or wrong in our actions, what is good or bad, is love. Ask yourself if your actions reflect the Love that is God. If they do, and if you genuinely do unto others as you would have them do unto you, you can be assured that your behavior is good and you are on the right path.

I release to you my free will, my Beautiful Lord.

Please take it! I need only You. Let me experience
the Love That is Heaven—Your very
Presence in the quietness of my soul.

You are my Teacher, my Lover, my Judge,
my Physician, my Father.

I love You.

ALL YOU NEED IS LOVE

Walk into any stage magic performance, and you will be surrounded by striking visuals and props that draw you into a rich set of feelings. You will likely see smoke, bright lights, large screens, and drapes. The magician will speak and move in a particular way. Everything has been designed by the magician and his assistants to set a tone—to lull you into being open to the tricks you are about to witness.

From experiences like this, all of us know the power of creating a powerful setting. Away from the stage, however, we often fail to think about the setting we are creating in our own lives. What tone are you setting with your life right now? If people observed your home, your behavior, your speech, what message would they take from it? Christianity teaches that you can use your life as a powerful way of setting a tone, for yourself and others, about your love for God and your belief in the connection between death and life.

Eternity and the Here and Now

When Christians speak of *eternity*, we face the limitations of our language and our powers of imagination. We typically think of time as the unfolding of one day, then another, continuing forever, and eternity as something like "a very long time." Scripture and tradition are very clear, however, that eternity relates to a different kind of existence where our usual ways of existence will be transformed.

The task of being Christian is sometimes a daunting one. We're required to love our enemies, protect life, and preserve truth. In addition, we are asked to make sure that others know we are Christians by our love (Jn 13:35). We've all heard about this, and I suspect that all of us ultimately agree that we ought to do so. But the questions still remain: What exactly are we to do when we minister to and evangelize our brothers and sisters? How do we bring God into our lives and the lives of others?

The beauty and genius of Christianity is that it is not a theoretical cloud of ideas existing in some perfect and nonexistent universe. Instead, it is a God-centered philosophy of life in a very concrete world, which leads us to the Source of Life. A life centered around the Church's sacraments is sufficient, if done properly, to bring us to a state of sanctity. But, in so doing, the Holy Spirit will lead us to spread the joy we receive as part of God's grace. The world tries to misdirect us with material possessions, slowly sapping us of our time, energy, and resources, but we must reject this and instead answer Christ's call.

These works are good, but they are not "good works" in the sense of actions that arise purely from our own initiative—they flow out of our love for God. In the light of God's love, we can become the conduit through which God enters our lives and the lives of others. I've listed here fifteen things for Christians to do to minister to and evangelize themselves and others. Most of these are simple tasks that don't require a lot of money or time— just the willingness to allow the light of eternity to shine into your daily existence. Consider them in recreating and renewing your life in Christ:

1
Invite others to church.

G. K. Chesterton once asked in defense of Catholicism, "Is one religion as good as another? Is one horse in the Derby as good as another?" If you are proud and grateful to be a Christian, one should behave that way. Invite non-Christians to a Mass or to other church activities. They might very well be waiting for that gentle nudge in order to reconnect with or learn more about the Faith.

2
Attend pet blessings.

There is nothing like a church parking lot full of furry, feathered, and scaled creatures to stop traffic. I consider the annual Blessing of the Animals on St. Francis of Assisi's feast day to be one of the Church's best evangelization outreach programs. Invite your neighbors, Christian or otherwise, to the annual blessing. You'll be sure to open up a few lines of communication with them.

3
Bless your children.

Contrary to popular belief, every Christian has the ability to bless. Every blessing originates in God. Bless your children every day in the silence of your heart. Ask their guardian angels to watch over them. If their angels aren't listening to you, how exactly are they earning their keep?

4
Practice night prayer/recollection.

The kids are in bed. The dishes are done. The cat's been let out. The pressures of the day are slipping away. In those few, free moments you have before going to sleep for the evening, take the time to consider how you have affected those around you and how successful, or unsuccessful, you have been in being Christ's light to the world. With God's help, resolve to be a better person.

5

Mend fences.

I have a strict rule by which I live. I might very well have the best excuses to justify my anger at some of the more egregious people in my life but come Advent and Lent, all bets are off. If you can't forgive your enemies at Christmas and Easter, what use is it to be Christian? And if they refuse your overtures for peace, there's always another holiday coming up in a few months.

6

Give Christian presents.

Instead of giving expensive electronics and other stuff that migrates to the back of the closet only to wait for the next garage sale, consider giving crucifixes, icons, spiritual treatises, religious statues and even car blessing plaques. How about planting a rose garden dedicated to Jesus or the Virgin Mary? These are all enduring gifts that will never go out of style (or need batteries).

—————— 7 ——————

Pray every time an ambulance or police siren sounds.

I recall my kindergarten teacher telling my class to do exactly this. I was surprised to find out later on that this was a common Christian school experience. I was once asked by a catechumen how many times Christians pray per day. I told her that we should pray whenever someone needs our prayers and gave her the example of the sirens being a request for urgent prayers. I saw a light grow in her eyes as she thought about what I had told her. From time to time even today, she mentions how she still prays for emergency victims and our first responders.

—————— 8 ——————

Cross yourself when passing a church.

This is a simple and ancient tradition. St. Ignatius of Antioch, a first-century patristic author, specifically chronicled the use of the sign of the cross among ancient Christians. St. John of Damascus, a seventh-century Doctor of the Church, also wrote that the sign of the cross distinguishes us as God's people just as *mezuzuhim* do for Jews. In many ways, it's a sign of humility. I've frequently found myself avoiding crossing myself because I didn't want to attract attention from strangers around me. It was at that point when I realized that it would be an excellent opportunity for me to witness to Christ's love and His presence in our lives.

9
Say grace before meals, both in public eateries and at home.

Generally speaking, I take seriously Christ's admonition about praying away from prying eyes (Mt 6:6) but when you do so for the sake of others rather than for yourself, it seems like a gentle and efficacious means by which to evangelize. Like other overt public displays of piety, this can be a bit humbling but it is a magnificent opportunity to give to God that which is His (Mt 22:16–22).

10
Place a cross or icon in every room.

This is an old-fashioned act of piety but one that can be reimbued with meaning and beauty. As gentle reminders of your own faith and of God's presence in your life, they will show houseguests the depth of your faith and its importance in your family's life.

11

Celebrate your *onomastico.*

Having grown up in an Italian household, I was surprised to find that many other Christians generally do not celebrate their *onomastico* or "name saint day." In a traditional Italian household, one's *onomastico* was more important than even one's birthday. A little bit of research will turn up the feast days of everyone in your family. Celebrate them in a special way with a party and attending Mass. Afterwards, ask the celebrant for a blessing for your children in honor of their patron saint.

12

Volunteer as a family and as individuals.

Faith without good works is dead (Jas 2:12–26). It is useless to speak of prayer and your love of God if you are disinterested in human suffering. What more perfect way to let the world know that you are a follower of Christ other than loving and caring for those that can not hope to repay you (Jn 13:35)?

13

Start a prayer corner.

If you have the space in your home, reserving a corner for prayer and mediation is an excellent way to bring Christ into your home and your life.

Other than serving as a reminder to always bring Christ into your heart, it can also serve as a starting point for the curious who visit your home.

—— 14 ——
Keep a prayer journal.
Most of us are not blessed with such incredible memories that we can recall the progress we've made or the problems we've encountered as we develop in our spiritual lives over the years. It is therefore imperative to keep a record of our experiences in prayer and our personal thoughts about God and our Faith. Such an exercise is a tremendous investment in time and energy but your journal can become an incredible resource when you review it from time to time.

—— 15 ——
Remember to trust in God.
If you recognize God's creatorship of the universe, who can be against you(Rom 8:31)? Let us be grateful for God's gifts. We can have courage in God's presence, because we are sure that He hears us if we ask Him for anything that is according to His will. Do not fear to knock and the door will be opened to you (Mt 7:7). Your trust in God will be one of the most powerful testimonies you can offer to others. We diminish as God increases.

I yearn to see You, Lord.
I search the faces of those around me to find You.
I seek the Love that You used to create us all.
For those I meet on the path to find You,
help me be Your eyes and Your hands
so that they too would see You in me.

KEEPING VIGIL WITH OUR DEAD

Happy are those who mourn; God will comfort them!
—Matthew 5:4

In all shows, including stage magic, performance choices matter. You'll see the magician use special exaggerated movements. You'll hear various phrases, usually ones from mispronounced Latin that sound somewhat obscure and esoteric, like they just might be revealing some deeper truth. As "Abracadabra!" proves, though, it doesn't really matter much what the magical words and symbols mean. All that matters is that a certain effect is produced on the audience. The goal is for you to enjoy yourself.

Christianity has its own performances, but they are very different from the stage shows of the magician. The magician could just as easily change one word for another, one gesture for another, as long as the show remained entertaining. Christian ritual is much more than this. It conveys eternal truths and centuries of practice that connect believers from countless cultures around the globe. And among all our rituals, wakes and vigils hold a special place. All rituals rely on the fact that we are not merely intellects—we experience the world through our senses and our bodies. Wakes and vigils, like the Eucharist itself, don't merely rely on this fact—they explicitly teach and celebrate it. They are rituals that celebrate why we as human beings, souls and bodies, are able to enjoy rituals in the first place.

✠

The wake or vigil can be a cherished time to say goodbye to a loved one. It is sometimes the first opportunity for family and friends of the deceased to gather and console each other with reminiscences and prayer, and it is an integral part of the grieving process. The wake may be celebrated in the home of the deceased, in the funeral home, or in the church/oratory, and may last from a few hours to three days prior to the funeral Mass and burial. The ritual of the Catholic wake may take place at any time during these days. When an ordinary minister, that is, a bishop, priest, or deacon, is unavailable for the wake, one's pastor may designate a lay minister to preside at it. The tone of the wake is completely dependent upon the survivors. It might be a joyous occasion or a somber one.

Traditionally, the Catholic Church had required a suitable amount of time to lapse between the moment of death and the actual internment of the body, especially where death has occurred unexpectedly. Historically, this was to assure that the deceased was actually dead. Today there are different advantages. Many Christian families live very far from each other. Waiting a few days before the actual funeral and interment allows far-flung family members to assemble and to make suitable arrangements. Just as importantly, the three days allow the survivors to say goodbye.

The custom of attending or waiting with the corpse is ancient. The Christian observance is traditionally accompanied by the singing or reciting of psalms. Throughout the Middle Ages, relays of monks and nuns would attend the corpse so that it was never left unattended and the soul unprayed for. The Office for the Dead (the prayer cycle to be said for the repose of the soul) originally developed from the practice of passing the night reciting psalms beside the corpse.

Some lay Catholic communities will allow a person to be buried in ceremonial garb. These groups include the Third Order Franciscans, Third Order Dominicans, Knights of Columbus, and Knights of Malta. Popes, bishops, priests, and deacons must be buried in their official vestments, including the vestments distinctive to their religious community. The deceased lay person should be dressed appropriately with their arms folded across their chest in the form of a cross, and a light is kept burning throughout the night. A small cross or a rosary beads is, if possible, placed in the deceased's hands, and the body should be blessed using holy water. Priests cannot serve as pall-bearers for deceased lay people, regardless of how eminent the deceased was in life. This prohibition stems from at least A.D. 1512. Priests may bear the coffin of their fellow priests, however.

Devotions such as the rosary are encouraged during the wake.

The Office for the Dead is also an excellent devotion that can be used during the wake. If eulogies are offered at the wake, comments should be restricted to the time immediately after the Prayer of Intercession. There is a great deal of recent discussion about eulogies. Some Church officials have remarked that they are becoming far too long, especially in the cases of the violent death of the young. While well-intentioned, this wordiness is often painful for the families and out of keeping with the intention of the wake. In addition, lay people often lack the training necessary to give an appropriate eulogy using sound Christian theology and spirituality.

For Visitors

It has been widely observed that people have forgotten or do not know how to dress appropriately at a wake. We don't dress modestly for the sake of the dead; we do so for the sake of the survivors. It's a matter of empathy, not etiquette. When we think of our own comfort before considering the emotional state of the bereaved, we are acting selfishly.

Funeral homes that serve the Christian community will usually have *prie-dieux* (kneelers) available for visitors who want to pray, including praying for the deceased. When a visitors' book is made available, it's customary to sign it. The mourners will take great pleasure in seeing a large number of names in the book. When greeting the mourners, you should imbue your words with comfort and hope. At this point, mourners are often in a tentative and weakened emotional and spiritual state. It is incumbent upon you as the visitor to respect this. It is customary for the family and friends of the deceased to print holy cards to serve as reminders of the deceased. These cards will inevitably include such information as the person's dates of birth and death. The front of the card will usually include a scriptural verse or a religious icon.

Don't ask the survivors if you can bring food—take it upon yourself to simply bring some for their sake. It will never go to waste, and your generosity will spare the bereaved yet another concern. They have more than enough to worry about at this point.

Requiem/Funeral Mass

The Funeral Mass is the most important of the Christian liturgies surrounding death. There are two common misconceptions about this Mass. First, you might hear it referred to as the Memorial Mass, but this is misleading. Every Mass is a memorial—a memorial of the Paschal mystery. Second, strictly speaking, Christians don't celebrate the resurrection of the dead at the funeral. We believe, instead, that the resurrection of the body will come at the end of time.

The Church teaches that the Eucharist is at the heart of the Christian death (CCC 1689). The Eucharist is the fullest expression of our communion with those who have gone before us. Despite being deceased, one is still a living member of the Body of Christ; we refer to this as being part of the *Communion of Saints* (CCC 1689). This view is based in part on Paul's Letter to the Corinthians, where Paul describes the Church as being united in Christ:

Christ is like a single body, which has many parts; it is still one body, even though it is made up of different parts. In the same way, all of us, whether Jews or Gentiles, whether slaves or free, have been baptized into the one body by the same Spirit and we have all been given the one Spirit to drink. (1 Cor 12:12–13)

St. Cyril of Jerusalem (A.D. 350), an early patristic writer, echoes this view in one of his lectures:

We mention those who have fallen asleep: first the patriarchs, prophets, apostles, and martyrs, that through their prayers and supplications God would receive our petition. (*Catechetical Lecture* 23:9)

The Funeral Mass allows the family and friends of the deceased to mourn the loss, celebrate his life, and hope for his or her entry into God's presence. The Funeral Mass offers you solace and hope for your own future as well. Christians believe their bodies will be resurrected, glorified, and reunited with their souls at the End of Times.

This is one of the distinctive aspects of Christian teaching. In *The Tibetan Book of the Dead*, as in many forms of Buddhism, the body is a shell, an empty husk that is easily discarded for that of another human being or, in some instances, another creature altogether. Christians look at life and the afterlife differently. We do not see matter (including the body) as an impediment. Rather, we enjoy it. Our saints and mystics constantly refer to the fact that we can see God in His handiwork. St. Francis of Assisi saw God in nature. St. Don Bosco heard God in the laughter of children. St. Albert the Great saw God in the process of learning and in unraveling the secrets of the universe. As Louis Pasteur said, "Science brings men nearer to God. The more I study nature, the more I stand amazed at the Creator's work." Death, then, does not mean the liberation of spirit from body. It means a new phase of our existence because we are being called back to God.

What can you expect, then, when it is time for your own funeral?

To my Sister Death. Thank you. It is through your embrace that I may see my Lord. As I contemplate my eventual end, I pray to the Lord Who created us both that I may be found worthy when you come to collect me. I pray for a happy and blessed end so that I may give glory to God both in my life and in my demise.

HEAVEN OR HELL?

At the beginning of our journey, I invited you to reflect on how it would feel to be lying in your own coffin. Such a meditation has been used by countless people through the centuries as a way of contemplating the reality of death and the meaning of our choices in life. At the same time, it is not quite the way things will happen. Unlike many pagan traditions that represent the soul as remaining on earth after the death of the body, Christianity teaches something different. The body and soul will one day be reunited in the Final Judgment, but in the meantime, the soul will not have time to worry too much about the body or the opinion other people have of it.

While many Christians are familiar with the Final Judgment that takes place at the end of time, there is also a judgment that takes places at the very moment of death. We refer to this as the Particular Judgment. It is at this moment or state that your actions during your life are weighed. At the Particular Judgment, the virtuous who die in a state of grace are immediately rewarded with the Beatific Vision, while those who have need for final purgation are assigned to Purgatory. Those who refuse to accept love in their life are, sorrow-fully, relegated to Hell, which they themselves have already chosen. Those who choose Hell are destined to remain there forever.

If Hell was just a place like you see depicted in cartoons, full of people dressed in tatters, being ruled over by a devil wearing red spandex wield-ing a pitchfork, at least there would be an absurd side to entertain you as you languished there for eternity. Hell is by far worse than that, however. While it is worse than we can ever imagine, we have some experiences of Hell on earth. Imagine a time when you were the most depressed, lonely, and dejected you've ever felt. That seems to me to be Hell. When we are betrayed by friends and unwanted by family . . . that is Hell. When we have neither options nor hope . . . that is Hell. If Heaven is the presence of God, then Hell is the horror of rejecting Him, of being completely alone in an uncaring and purposeless universe.

The great medieval Italian poet Dante, in his *Divine Comedy,* described Hell not as a prison into which God condemns those who have sinned but rather a state of existence that is the natural end of one's free choice of living without regard to love. This is not to say that Dante populated Heaven and Purgatory only with holy people. He took great pains to describe Purgatory and Heaven as places replete with sinners—reformed, occasional sinners. Hell, on the other hand, is a place in which the selfishly and unwisely unrepentant imprison themselves, despite God's perpetual love, grace, and call to union and holiness

Hell is a howling, desperate emptiness that threatens to overwhelm us in our most distressed, loneliest, and most frightening moments.

It is so horrible that we would be tempted to wish for those physical pains popularly conceived of which had been part of the traditional perception of Hell. The only difference between the Hell that is experienced on this side of eternity and those on the other side is that ours here is temporary, and God always holds out hope for us. The other side is much more intense and destructive because there is no hope of God's love whatsoever, just as the greatest joys of our lives are only a mere shadow of the experience of the Beatific Vision.

> *Lord of Life. Lord of Love. Forgive me my sins. Remove from me my heart of stone and replace it with one of flesh. My sins weigh heavily upon my soul and I am in the depths of despair over them. Cleanse me. Heal me. Show me how to love You.*

THE ASTOUNDING GRACE
OF PURGATORY

As Christians, we believe that if Hell is not your soul's destination, then after the Particular Judgment, you will quite likely find yourself in purgatory. It is widely believed that, with the exception of a few blessed souls who have lived heroically virtuous lives and died in a state of grace, purgatory is the soul's destination.

Purgatory is one of the most beautiful and misunderstood features of the afterlife. It is often seen as a tentative, intermediate state between Heaven and Hell, suggesting that a soul in Purgatory stands an equal chance of landing in one or the other. This is wildly inaccurate. Purgatory is best understood as the vestibule to Heaven. If your soul is in Purgatory, you are blessed, because you have been judged worthy enough to be forgiven of your sins. A soul in purgatory will never find itself in Hell.

Dante and the Paradox of Purgatory

In Dante's *Purgatory*, the poet Virgil responds to the author's question with a rich description of purgatory.

These lines beautifully capture the paradoxical nature of purgatory—as a place that pulls us away from the selfish pleasures that usually give us happiness, yet as we remain there, we become ever more happy.

> But, if it pleaseth thee, I fain would learn
> How far we have to go; for the hill rises
> Higher than eyes of mine have power to rise.
>
> And he to me: "This mount is such, that ever
> At the beginning down below 'tis tiresome,
> And aye the more one climbs, the less it hurts.
>
> Therefore, when it shall seem so pleasant to thee,
> That going up shall be to thee as easy
> As going down the current in a boat,
>
> Then at this pathway's ending thou wilt be;
> There to repose thy panting breath expect;
> No more I answer; and this I know for true."
>   (canto 4, lines 87–98; Longfellow's translation)

Dante's *Divine Comedy* is not a formal part of Christian teaching, but it offers many challenging and inspiring ideas about what the afterlife will be like and how we can live today in a way that honors it and prepares us for it.

In Mother Mary of St. Austin's *The Divine Crucible of Purgatory*, she describes those in Purgatory as being in a state of grace, which means they will eventually be purified and enter into God's presence. In a sense, if you are in Purgatory, you've already "made it." The purification your soul goes through is meant to satisfy sins committed in your life. The theology for this point is derived from Matthew's Gospel:

> Anyone who says something against the Son of Man can be forgiven; but whoever says something against the Holy Spirit will not be forgiven—now or ever. (Mt 12:32)

This passage suggests that some sins (mortal sins) land people in Hell, while others (venial sins) are forgivable but still need to be expiated. Thus, Purgatory is a sign of great hope, of God's inconceivable love for even great sinners. It is not a place for those who failed to impress God adequately.

Pain and suffering in this world are a result not of God's vengeance or wrath. Instead, they are a natural result of our free will. The possession of free will carries with it a heavy price. But with pain and suffering come empathy for and communion with all who suffer. Without pain, we might become sociopaths, unconcerned with the welfare of others. We would all be in our own perfect worlds, oblivious to and possibly acrimonious toward each other. This is the opposite of what

God asks of us, and it is hard to imagine a worse Hell on Earth.

St. Catherine of Genoa describes the need for such a purgative state in *Purgation and Purgatory*:[1]

> Look at gold: the more you melt it, the better it becomes; you could melt it until you had destroyed in it every imperfection. Thus does fire work on material things. The soul cannot be destroyed in so far as it is in God, but in so far as it is in itself it can be destroyed; the more it is purified, the more is self destroyed within it, until at last it is pure in God.

C. S. Lewis and the Desire to Be Cleansed

Another good discussion of the existence of Purgatory comes from someone whose religious denomination rejected it. C. S. Lewis, an Anglican, writes in his *Mere Christianity*:

> I believe in Purgatory. . . . The saved soul, at the very foot of the throne, begs to be taken away and cleansed. It cannot bear for a moment longer "With its darkness to affront that light." Religion has reclaimed Purgatory. Our souls demand Purgatory, don't they? Would it not break the heart if God said to us, "It is true . . . that your breath smells and your rags drip with mud and slime, but we are charitable here and no one will upbraid you with

---

these things, nor draw away from you. Enter into the joy"? Should we not reply, "With submission, Sir, and if there is no objection, I'd rather be cleaned first."—"It may hurt, you know."—"Even so, Sir."

This is a lovely testimony to the beautiful, positive value of Purgatory, as it represents a stage of existence, enlightenment, and moral purity that brings us ever closer to God.

I feel sorrow, not derision, for any theists who don't believe in Purgatory. If God doesn't judge, we are all perfect as we are. If we are perfect, we don't need God's grace. If we don't need God's grace, we are omnipotent and can do anything we want; thus we become our own standards of morality, making us omnibenevolent. When we eschew Purgatory, we make God redundant.

Purgatory is not some medieval addendum derived from speculative theology. Like the Trinity, Purgatory is a concept derived from scripture. Purgatory is a sign and promise of God's love and His grace, pointing to eternal glory. Learn to meditate more deeply on the beauty and hope of purgatory, the destiny of so many souls—perhaps including your own.

All of life is purgation, that is, the process of being spiritually cleansed; from the moment of conception to the moment of physical death, all is a healing of that First Sin that contaminates us all. My sin sloughs off at the touch of Your love, O Lord. Not from my own power or intention but only by your gracious bequest do I stand, humbled and cleansed before You. I am Yours.

THE FINAL CURTAIN

I have done my best in the race, I have run the full
distance, and I have kept the faith. And now there
is waiting for me the victory prize of being put right
with God, which the Lord, the righteous Judge, will
give me on that Day—and not only to me, but to all
those who wait with love for Him to appear.

—2 Timothy 4:7–8

In the eschaton, a word Christians use to mean
the end of time, all souls are called before God to
receive their Final Judgment. As we saw, souls in
Hell are destined to remain there forever. In this
consummation of all times, souls that have been
purged of their sins in Purgatory are released from
their spiritual debts and are welcomed into Heaven
to enjoy the beatific vision.

One problem Christians encounter when dis-
cussing the Final Judgment is how to reconcile
an omnibenevolent and omniscient God with his
function as Divine Judge. Would a loving God
judge us? Could a judging God love us? Such questions have been asked in every period of Christianity, from Augustine, Anselm, and Aquinas to
Teilhard de Chardin and Hans Urs von Balthasar.

The answer to both intertwined questions is Yes, but not in a way that many would immediately recognize and understand. The idea that God is extracting every last drop of punishment isn't what most Christians would accept and is not in keeping with Divine Revelation. According to Scripture and tradition, God loved us enough to sacrifice His own Son for our sakes. At the same time, God is not like a modern parent who decides that leniency is the best approach. If this were the case, what could we have learned while we were alive, if not to simply shrug every time someone does something morally outrageous and hurtful? If Christ died for us, it would seem that He had great moral expectations for us. If He didn't care what we did, it would have been preposterous for Him to undergo His passion.

Further, if God doesn't judge us and doesn't care what we do, we would instantly lose the right to demand better treatment and behavior from others. If God doesn't demand good behavior it of us, we have no right to demand it from others. If God isn't offering us an objective morality, what in God's Name is everyone complaining about when people mistreat us to get ahead, or just because they enjoy doing so?

The Good and the Wicked

The Final Judgment is referred to many times in Scriptures, but never so well described as in the Gospel of Matthew. Christ describes a scene where the good and the wicked are separated into two groups (Mt 25:31–46). The sole rule by which people are categorized is whether or not they were generous, loving, and kind to others.

It is common for people to think of God's judgment of us as harsh and exacting, but there is another way to think of the matter. Instead of God judging us, we judge ourselves. We already know the full extent of our evil. We all know how we treat others, and we know how we rationalize our own bad behavior. In our heart of hearts, each of us knows we are sinners. Some of us are ashamed of what we have done while others are exceedingly proud of the pain they've perpetrated upon others. Either way, our actual behavior becomes clear to us in the Light of Christ's all-encompassing Love.

Thus the simplest description of the Christian afterlife is an eternity of hatred of our own concocting in Hell or eternal, infinite, and unparalleled love in Heaven. Everyone may chose as they wish or, more accurately, we have already chosen our fate by how we lead our lives while we still have control over them. This reflects the Dantean image of Christ the Merciful Judge, Who judges not on your scrupulosity but on your capacity and willingness to reflect God's image in your soul. In this sense, it is not God Who judges and condemns, but you who condemn yourself by refusing to love your brothers and sisters, your fellow travelers on this earthly pilgrimage. This is, at the same time, heartening and frightening.

The Need to Forgive

Christ describes our penchant for hypocrisy in the Gospels:

Once there was a king who decided to check on his servants' accounts. He had just begun to do so when one of them was brought in who owed him millions of dollars. The servant did not have enough to pay his debt, so the king ordered him to be sold as a slave, with his wife and his children and all that he had, in order to pay the debt. The servant fell on his knees before the king. "Be patient with me," he begged, "and I will pay you everything!" The king felt sorry for him, so he forgave him the debt and let him go.

Then the man went out and met one of his fellow servants who owed him a few dollars. He grabbed him and started choking him. "Pay back what you owe me!" he said. His fellow servant fell down and begged him, "Be patient with me and I will pay you back!" But he refused; instead, he had him thrown into jail until he should pay the debt.

When the other servants saw what had happened, they were very upset and went to the king and told him everything. So he called the servant in. "You worthless slave!" he said. "I forgave you the whole amount you owed me, just because you asked me to. You should have had mercy on your fellow servant, just as I had mercy on you." The king was very angry, and he sent the servant to jail to be punished until he should pay back the whole amount." And Jesus concluded, "That is how My Father in Heaven will treat every one of you unless you forgive your brother from your heart." (Mt 18:23–35)

This parable is sobering. If we wish to be forgiven by God, we must be eager to forgive our enemies. Christ admonishes us throughout the Gospels to forgive and repent:

So if you are about to offer your gift to God at the altar and there you remember that your brother has something against you, leave your gift there in front of the altar, go at once and make peace with your brother, and then come back and offer your gift to God. (Mt 5:23–24)

In addition to forgiveness and repentance, Christ also warns us against hypocrisy, judgmental attitudes, and pride:

How terrible for you, teachers of the Law and Phari-
sees! You hypocrites! You lock the door to the Kingdom of Heaven in people's faces, but you yourselves
don't go in, nor do you allow in those who are trying to
enter! . . . "How terrible for you, blind guides! You
teach, 'If someone swears by the Temple, he isn't bound
by his vow; but if he swears by the gold in the Temple,
he is bound.' Blind fools! Which is more important,
the gold or the Temple which makes the gold holy?
You also teach, 'If someone swears by the altar, he isn't
bound by his vow; but if he swears by the gift on the
altar, he is bound.' How blind you are! Which is the
more important, the gift or the altar which makes the
gift holy? So then, when a person swears by the altar,
he is swearing by it and by all the gifts on it; and when
he swears by the Temple, he is swearing by it and by
God, Who lives there; and when someone swears by
Heaven, he is swearing by God's throne and by Him
Who sits on it. (Mt 23:13–33)

Hell is apparently a slippery slope that begins
on this side of eternity, and love is the only thing
that can slow and finally brake our descent. Before
you dismiss this idea as maudlin, Christian sen-
timentality, you should consider the countless
examples we have in the world of people who are
simultaneously mean-spirited and deeply loving.
Of course, there is no such a person. It's an all-or-
nothing deal. The more we love, the less we are

able to show cruelty. In this lifetime, we can either choose love or hatred, life or death, Heaven or Hell. Our limited human nature precludes the possibility of always being good, but if you are good, you will actively try to reduce the times you sin, and you will just as actively seek to redress the damage you've done.

Great Physician! Heal my Soul. Purify me so that I might love You as I love myself. Purify me so that I might love others as I love You. Show me my sins so that I might not judge others so harshly. Let me always see the good in others. Let others see the good in me as a reflection of You.

TASTING HEAVEN

May the angels lead you into paradise; may the martyrs greet you at your arrival and lead you into the
holy city, Jerusalem. May the choir of angels greet
you and like Lazarus, who once was a poor man, may
you have eternal rest.

—"In paradisum deducant te angeli"
(sung at the Rite of Commital)

An enormous Greek Orthodox priest dressed
completely in black stood before the Edicule (the
tomb of Christ) beaming welcome to every pilgrim
who came to visit. Its tiny door was too narrow and
too short to accommodate even a very short person,
forcing every pilgrim to bow and humble himself
or herself in order to enter. Only one pilgrim at a
time was allowed in the Edicule, giving him an
opportunity for private prayer. I bowed deeper
than was necessary, as the experience of being at
Christ's tomb was overwhelming. Inside the tiny
chapel was a large stone upon which Christ's body
was once laid and subsequently resurrected. This
is where it all began—the physical remains of the
single most important event in human and cosmic
history. I was shaking as I put out my hand to touch

the stone. At that moment, I recalled Rudolph Otto's description of God as *mysterium tremendens*, a mystery that is simultaneously fascinating and awesome. I was so excited about being at the site of my Lord's resurrection that I registered in my mind that I was breathing in, but I don't recall ever breathing out. For those moments in the Edicule, I felt perfectly at peace with both God and humanity. I stepped out of the Edicule reveling in the experience. The feeling was so palatable that I couldn't think of anything else; I truly didn't want to leave the church.

If meeting God is anything like the overwhelmingly joyous and humbling experience of stepping into the Holy Sepulchre, then we all have something truly wonderful to look forward to.

✠

For a magical illusion to work, either one by a legitimate stage performer or by someone trying to manipulate or defraud you, the magician must make sure that there are some things you don't get to see. They are hidden for effect, otherwise the illusion is destroyed. Heaven too is hidden from us, and for this reason, many people through the years have imagined that belief in the afterlife is merely another kind of magical thinking. But this overlooks the sublime nature of the afterlife. Heaven is esoteric because we simply lack the capacity to comprehend it. We can't just decide never to talk about it—it is too fascinating not to contemplate in some way—but we never can talk about it adequately. So Christ used parables, the New Testament authors used metaphors, and Christian mystics use poetic imagery and to convey a sense of what lies before us, just out of sight.

What pictures come to mind when you think about what Heaven will be like? Like many people, you may be filled with ideas we had as children—for example, fluffy clouds, harps, and naked cherubs. Throughout the Gospels, however, Christ speaks poignantly of Heaven, with rich allegorical and metaphorical imagery that engage our hearts and lives directly. Here are some of the striking images Christ offers you in the New Testament, and the parables from which they are drawn.

A Place of Truth

Heaven is a place where false beliefs and evil will not be tolerated (Sowed Field, Mt 13:24–30).

A Tree of Refuge

Heaven is an enormous tree that starts out very small and grows so large that it protects all who seek refuge under its branches (Mustard Seed, Mt 13:31–32).

A Place of Mystery and Joy

Heaven is a place of great joy and love that grows unexpectedly and mysteriously through the actions of the Holy Spirit (Yeast, Mt 13:33).

Vast Awareness

Heaven is an awareness of such impossible proportions that anyone who could grasp even a tiny bit of it would surely seek it out (Hidden Treasure, Pearl of Great Price, Mt 13:44–46).

A Just Place

Heaven is a selective place ruled by Divine Justice. It is a place ruled by both new and old traditions (Fishermen, Mt 13:47–48; Homeowner, Mt 13:52).

A Place that Mirrors Our Own Actions

Heaven is a place of ultimate justice, in which we will be judged by our own moral and ethical standards. That is, if we are unforgiving and ungenerous, God will be unforgiving and ungenerous to us (Selfish Servant, Mt 18:23–35).

A Place for the Humble

Heaven is a place of justice and generosity that requires us to be humble (Vineyard Workers, Mt 20:1–16).

A Place of Reward

Heaven is a place where one is rewarded for one's efforts (5000 Coins, Mt 25:14–30).

An Unexpected Place

Heaven is something that comes upon us unexpectedly, and thus we should be wary of apathy and general foolishness (Ten Virgins, Mt 25:1–13).

Ultimately, Heaven must always remain unexpected—we know so little about its exact features. In fact, there are limits to what we *can* know. Heaven is not a physical place, so all our images—even the most elevated and spiritualized images—are necessarily limited. Even the greatest of mystics struggle to describe Heaven. So, unlike *The Tibetan Book of the Dead*, with its vivid and very literal descriptions of colors, shapes, and dimensionality, no book can ever claim to paint a picture of Heaven. The Heaven we Christians believe in, and the glories that await you there when you come again into the presence of the Source of Life, can never be imagined or adequately described in words. The wonder of God and the joy of being in His presence—there is no language or science to describe this. We have only metaphor, poetry, and song. This does not mean, however, that Heaven is vague or unreal. It is the most real of all human experiences. You can be assured that when you arrive there, you will be united with Christ and dwell in communion with the saints.

I've known Hell, Father. Show me Heaven.

*Show me Your Face. Make me thrill
at the sound of Your Name.*

*Let me see You in all whom I meet. Let me hear Your echoes
in Nature. Let me witness Your handiwork in creation.
Pull me into Holy Presence. There I will taste Heaven.*

DAYS WE ARE ONE FAMILY

Listen to this secret truth: we shall not all die, but
when the last trumpet sounds, we shall all be changed
in an instant, as quickly as the blinking of an eye. For
when the trumpet sounds, the dead will be raised,
never to die again, and we shall all be changed. For
what is mortal must be changed into what is immortal; what will die must be changed into what cannot
die. So when this takes place, and the mortal has
been changed into the immortal, then the scripture
will come true: "Death is destroyed; victory is complete!" "Where, Death, is your victory? Where, Death,
is your power to hurt?" Death gets its power to hurt
from sin, and sin gets its power from the Law. But
thanks be to God Who gives us the victory through
our Lord Jesus Christ! So then, my dear friends, stand
firm and steady. Keep busy always in your work for
the Lord, since you know that nothing you do in the
Lord's service is ever useless.

—1 Corinthians 15:51–58

"I know my grandmother is in Heaven looking
down on me . . . protecting me."

Even the greatest of skeptics would be moved
by this statement of faith from the mouth of a

child. These simple words point to a fundamental truth of our faith. Death is not the end; it is only a beginning.

A Catholic friend of mine converted to the Baptist faith because he married a young Baptist woman. He confided in me many years later that he wanted to be buried as a Catholic in a Catholic cemetery but wasn't sure whom he should approach. He worried that the request was at odds with his decision to convert.

I explained to him that a consecrated Catholic cemetery was an extension of a parish. A person hopefully will choose to live his life with us but, if circumstances don't allow, he is welcome to spend eternity with us in our cemeteries.[1]

All Christians are united in Christ. If not, there seems to be little use in believing in Him, the sole origin and single goal of all believers. This union of all Christians, the living and the dead, is referred to as the Communion of Saints even though the word "saint" otherwise refers to deceased Christians who lived exemplary lives and enjoy the Beatific Vision. Together, the living and the dead assist each other in their shared prayers since we are united as a single body which has Christ as its head (Eph 1:10; Col 2:19). There are three groups in the Christian community:

Ecclesia Militans

This is the Church Militant, those Christians who are still living. Although the Latin word *militans* can refer to being a soldier, it can also mean "to struggle" or "to make an effort." Christians on earth, the Church Militant, are still struggling against sin.

Ecclesia Triumphans

This is the "Church Triumphant," those Christians who have died and are now enjoying the Beatific Vision (i.e., who are already in Heaven, prior to the eschaton). Christians in Heaven have "triumphed" over sin.

Ecclesia Penitens

This third group is the "Church Suffering," those Christians who are presently in Purgatory. They are also described as the "Church Expectant" (*Ecclesia Expectans*) because they have been saved but are awaiting complete purgation of their sins.

Though Christians may be separated from each other by time, space, and even death (Lk 16:26), we remain united to each other in the Church and support each other in prayer. The souls in Purgatory are looking forward to happiness and are, in fact, praying for us just as we pray for them. We are not long separated from those we love. We worry about each other despite the veil of death that separates us. We should pray for them just as they pray for us. Surely, they also long to be reunited with us as we do with them. To disregard those who have passed before us seems unnatural. Our sympathies, emotions, and memories always tell us that there is a connection between us and them. My compassion for my ancestors is as important to me as my compassion for those who follow me. Even some atheists acknowledge this concern. Many wonder about the future and hope to leave a healthy and peaceful world for humanity once we have died.

My dead relatives and friends are as present to me as they were when they lived and breathed upon the earth. I miss having conversations with them, but I still feel them in my heart. Some believe that the dead should no longer concern us, but why should we be asked to curtail our compassion? When you are truly compassionate, you cannot restrict your compassion any more than you can restrict the pull of gravity.

If those in Heaven are truly holy people, it follows that we are allowed to approach them to ask their prayers. (They cannot grant prayers, of course, as only God can do this.) The scriptures teach us: "So then, confess your sins to one another and pray for one another, so that you will be healed. The prayer of a good person has a powerful effect" (Jas 5:16).

This is the basis of saint veneration among Christians. We do not worship the saints—we ask them to join us in prayer. Further, if souls in Purgatory are blessed to have the opportunity to be cleansed of their remaining sins, are they not in greater union with God than we are here on earth? If this is so, then we can also rely upon their prayers as well. We pray for them and they pray for us. And all of us rely upon the grace of God.

Our brothers and sisters in Heaven, those in Purgatory, and those living among us now are one community; we are one in Christ. Christ's Body cannot be disjointed. Our Faith teaches that we, the living, are truly connected to the dead. For this reason, we praise the actions of our martyrs and other saints, both ancient and modern, and pray to have the courage and faith to emulate them.

Think back to the wake and funeral. If we were meant to simply forget about the dead, why bother with a funeral at all? If the soul was the only important part of a person, why not simply throw the empty corpse onto the garbage heap? We treat the dead body with respect in order to maintain respect for that person, not just his memory. If this is true, then it follows that the hope of resurrection in Christ requires us to maintain the deceased in our community, the Communion of Saints.

> May the angels lead you into Paradise;
> may the martyrs come to welcome you
> and take you to the Holy City,
> the new and eternal Jerusalem.
> —Rite for Christian Burial

Though we can pray for the deceased at any time, the Church reserves the month of November to pray for the deceased beginning with the first days of the month, All Saints Day (November 1) and All Souls Day (November 2). All Saints Day commemorates the Church Triumphant, the Blessed in Heaven, and All Souls Day commemorates the Church Suffering, the Blessed in Purgatory. Halloween (October 31) is included in this triple feast because it is the vigil for All Saints Day.

Halloween

Isia moriendo renascor ("In death I am reborn")
> —motto of the French village Èze

I've always enjoyed Halloween. It's tailor-made for professional magicians. Picture all the magical iconography—the pointy-hatted witches, Merlin, the magically animated zombies, and other uncanny, mystical happenings. Picture too how important death and dying are in the costumes and decorations—the skulls and skeletons, the depictions of blood. What you may not realize, however, is that this holiday is also a richly Christian one, and therefore it represents a remarkable encounter among magic, death, and faith.

Symbolically and historically, Halloween is often associated with the supernatural, pagan views of death, and other spooky ideas, but the evolution of the holiday from its ancient origins to its current form is interesting. It's been said that Halloween was originally a Celtic holiday called "Samhain." This is not completely accurate. It is true that the ancient Celts celebrated a minor holiday on October 31 dedicated to the harvest, but they celebrated a festival on the last day of almost every month of the year. In the Christian calendar, November 1 is All Saints Day, or All Hallows Day, a day dedicated to remembering those who have passed before us. The word *Halloween* is the abbreviated form of the phrase All Hallow's Eve, the evening vigil celebration of the next day. Christianity continued the Jewish custom of commencing a holiday celebration on the night before the festival. The holiday to honor All Saints had originally been celebrated on May 13, but in A.D. 731, Pope Gregory III moved it to November 1 in commemoration of the founding of the All Saints Chapel in St. Peter's in Rome. In A.D. 998, St. Odilo, the abbot of France's Cluny Monastery, added a celebration on November 2 dedicated to praying for the souls of all the faithful departed and not just the saints. Not long afterwards, the holiday was added to the universal calendar.

By the time these festive reforms were instituted, Europe had long been Christianized. Despite what you may hear from people who call themselves modern-day neopagans or witches, Halloween was not a way to accommodate pagans or bully them into becoming Christian. The practice of dressing in costumes for All Souls Day originated in France during the fourteenth and fifteenth centuries. During the Black Death epidemics of medieval Europe, artists would depict *la Dance Macabre* (The Dance of Death) on cemetery walls and coffins. Images would depict the devil or Death leading a ring of the recently deceased into a tomb. Eventually, a custom arose in France of reenacting *la Dance Macabre* on All Souls Day with people dressing up as the dead. It was believed that the demons out and about on that night would be fooled by the masked party-goers and move on in search for a place devoid of their colleagues and co-diabolics.

Guy Fawkes Day (November 5) commemorates the unsuccessful Catholic uprising in Britain known as the Gunpowder Plot that sought to blow up Parliament and overthrow King James's anti-Catholic government. It was celebrated by small children who would don masks and go about begging "a penny for the Guy," the hapless keeper of the gunpowder intended for the revolution. Adult revelers would demand beer and cakes. Tricks and treats, indeed! The custom of dressing in masquerade and asking for small presents migrated easily to All Hollows Eve. Halloween is thus steeped in Christian theology and piety—and besides, it's just so much fun. We couldn't ask for a more perfect synthesis of devotion and festivity.

All Saints Day

The smoke of the burning incense went up with the prayers of God's people from the hands of the angel standing before God.

—Revelations 8:4

All Saints Day, also known as All Hallows or Hallowmas, is celebrated on November 1, the day after Halloween. It is meant to honor all of the saints in Heaven, known and otherwise. The Catholic Church has recognized approximately 15,000 canonized saints. Other Churches such as the Orthodox Church have an extensive list as well. All Saints Day is a Holy Day of Obligation for Catholics.

As we have seen, the saints are holy men and women, some clerics, some religious, and many lay people, whose lives the Church has investigated and found worthy of imitation because of their lives of heroic virtue. Seeking out miracles performed by the intercession of these individuals, we can come to an assurance that they are indeed in Heaven. If such is the case, they are excellent intercessors before God on our behalf. The interests a saint had in life can become her patronal field in the afterlife. To take an example from my own field, St. John Don Bosco is considered the Patron of Stage Magicians because he used magic tricks to delight the children in his care. St. Teresa of Ávila is the Patron of Bodily Ills because of the tremendous suffering she experience throughout her life. Since St. Denis was martyred in Paris, he is the patron of that city. Because of scriptural passage of St. Peter the Apostle being associated with the keys to the kingdom, he is considered the Patron of Security Guards, Locksmiths, and Bouncers. The Venerable Matt Talbot had difficulty overcoming his addiction to alcohol, and so recovering alcoholics ask Matt to keep them in his prayers. Since St. Francis of Assisi was so fond of animals, veterinarians, zookeepers, and dogcatchers have taken him as their patron. Since Gabriel the Archangel carried God's message to Mary about Christ's birth, philatelists, who are also interested in things that carry messages, took him as their patron. There are so many saints in the Catholic Church that each day of the liturgical calendar carries at least thirty feast days.

All Souls Day

> For God has already placed Jesus Christ as the one and only foundation, and no other foundation can be laid. Some will use gold or silver or precious stones in building on the foundation; others will use wood or grass or straw. And the quality of each person's work will be seen when the Day of Christ exposes it. For on that Day fire will reveal everyone's work; the fire will test it and show its real quality. If what was built on the foundation survives the fire, the builder will receive a reward. But if your work is burnt up, then you will lose it; but you yourself will be saved, as if you had escaped through the fire.
>
> —1 Corinthians 3:11–15

The day after All Saints Day is All Souls Day. The feast commemorates all those faithful who have died but are still in Purgatory. It is a day to remember and offer prayers up on behalf of all of the faithful departed. In many Christian cultures such as Italy, France, Poland, and Mexico, this is a day that mourners will visit the graves of the dead. Though it is not a Holy Day of Obligation like the preceding feast, many Christians will attend Mass in honor of the deceased members of their families.

When you too have departed, those who live will use these days to remember you and souls like you, just as you will remember the living. Death is a transition but not a rupture, for nothing can sever the community of saints.

Merciful Lord of All, I thank You for the realization that I am never alone in this universe. The souls that have gone before me are never lost to me. They are as present to me as are the souls that come into contact with me every day of my life. As they are not lost, I know that neither am I.

THE WONDROUS PILGRIMAGE TOWARD LOVE

Go forth, Christian soul, from this world in the name
of God the Almighty Father, Who created you, in the
name of Jesus Christ, Son of the Living God, Who
suffered for you, in the name of the Holy Spirit, Who
was poured out upon you. May you live in peace this
day, may your home be with God in Zion, with Mary,
the Virgin Mother of God, with Joseph and all the
angels and saints.

—Prayers of Commendation
(spoken as the time of death approaches)

Life is a pilgrimage. We move from confusion
and ignorance, dragging with us unnecessary,
self-imposed burdens and coming to our natural
end, the thing that has motivated us from the
beginning: Love Itself. In the unexamined periods
of our lives, we reject that which is good, whole-
some, and life-sustaining and instead, seek out
worthless, selfish ends. The relentless pursuit of
personal satisfaction at the expense of all others
is spiritually costly. As Scripture warns us: "I am
now giving you the choice between life and death,
between God's blessing and God's curse, and I call

Heaven and earth to witness the choice you make. Choose life" (Dt 30:19).

What choice have you made?

Love: The Soul's Single Hope

Throughout this book, I've attempted to portray our earthly pilgrimage as a movement from faithlessness to faith and from death to life. Death not only refers to the termination of our physical functions. It can also refer to our refusal to recognize the importance of love in our lives. Thus, if you realize the futility and painful emptiness of your existence and that of others, you can be moved to recognize love as the soul's single hope. Love cures us of our restlessness and self-hatred. Love is in fact our only *raison d'être*; it is the meaning of our lives. It saves us from our worst selves and makes monsters into human beings. By recognizing the meaning, importance, and Source of love, we come to life. Food, shelter, medicine, and clothing are essential for physical life, but a person who is given only these things and nothing else becomes materialistic, and excessively loves himself and hates others. Even an education does not bring him satisfaction and inner peace. A person who is shown and shows love, however, comes to recognize his true humanity. Your very existence will lead you to love others.

✠

Whenever I perform the illusion of sawing a woman in half, I always make sure I look at the faces of my audience members. Some stage magic is simple, fun buffoonery, but some, like this particular illusion, incorporate and depend upon some kind of terror and suspense. We all know rationally that the woman is in no danger whatsoever and that everything will work out. But there is a non-rational part of each of us that I enjoy observing from my vantage point as the stage performer. While she live? Will she die? Those two sides are balanced delicately in my audience's mind for that brief fraction of a second. And that terror is similar to what many people feel about their own lives— Will I live? Will I die? What will death be like? The prospect can be terrifying.

For Christians, however, death holds no terror. You can be confident that God will do with your soul what is appropriate and right. Such is the nature of faith. Such is the nature of the Faith. Such is the nature of our God.

Death holds no terror for you as a Christian. If it did, Christ's sacrifice was in vain. God's love and mercy are as incomprehensible as they are boundless. Confident in this belief, you can steadfastly and courageously rely upon His mercy, despite your sins, despite your past and despite your failings, to approach Him in prayer. As a Christian, you can prepare for your final hours, and for subsequent eternity, through compassion and humility; by caring for others more than yourself. Acting in this way fills the incomprehensible void in you. And by filling it with love, your soul survives death because it is made in God's image and He is the source of your love. Certainly, Nature has not provided you with the ability to fill that infinite void in you. As Fr. Lorenzo Albacete often says, only something infinite, the Source of Love Itself, will suffice. That source of healing is God Himself. It is through love for one another that God reveals Himself to you. And with His love, you have everything you need in life. From this realization, you come to thankfulness, and this thankfulness leads to love. Love leads to joy. Joy leads us to faith. And faith leads to grace. Grace brings you to Heaven.

"It is finished!" (Jn 19:30)

Prayer for Acceptance of Death

My Beautiful Lord,
If it is Your decision
to call me to Your side this day (night),
I pray that You grant me Your mercy
for my many sins, faults and failings.
I accept the pains, losses and sorrows
that are part and parcel of that death
in reparation for my many sins,
for the souls suffering in Purgatory
and for Your greater glory.

My life is Yours.
Amen.

OFFICE OF THE DEAD

The great Physician of souls, Who is the ready libera-
tor, not of you alone, but of all who are enslaved by
sin, is ready to heal your sickness. From Him come
the words, it was His sweet and saving lips that said,
"They that be whole need not a physician but they
that are sick. . . . I am not come to call the righteous
but sinners to repentance."
     —St. Basil the Great, Letter to a Fallen Virgin

As startling as the expression is, the Office of
the Dead refers to a set of prayers in the Catholic
Church's Liturgy of the Hours which were originally written in the seventh or eighth century. It
is recited for the repose of the soul of the deceased,
very much like the Jewish Kaddish. In addition to
being used for memorials for individuals who have
died, it is also used on All Souls' Day (November
2) to pray for the souls in Purgatory. The Office
of the Dead, like the other prayers of the Liturgy
of the Hours, is composed of invitatory prayer,
two or three psalms, hymns, canticles, scriptural
readings, antiphons, intercessions, the Our Father,
and a final blessing. Unlike the other prayers of
the Liturgy of the Hours, the Office of the Dead

is composed of only the major hours of Vespers, Matins, and Lauds. Each of the psalms prayed in The Office for the Dead ends with the same refrain: "Eternal rest give unto them, O Lord and let perpetual light shine upon them," in the place of the Glory Be. The following is the Morning Prayer (Lauds) of the Office of the Dead. It can also be used as is for All Souls' Day. If prayed in a group of people, one half of the group should read a single passage to which the other half will respond with the next passage. (The texts for the Office of the Dead were taken with the kind permission from Martin Kochanski's website Universalis.com. Universalis is dedicated to exposing Christians to their prayer heritage in the form of the Liturgy of the Hours.)

VESPERS (EVENING PRAYER)

O God, come to my assistance.
Response: O Lord, make haste to help me.

† *Glory be to the Father and to the Son and to the Holy Spirit, as it was in the beginning, is now, and ever shall be, world without end. Amen. Alleluia.*

Psalm 120 (121)

The guardian of the people

The Lord will guard you from every evil. May the Lord guard your soul. I shall lift my eyes to the hills: where is my help to come from? My help will come from the Lord, Who made Heaven and earth. He will not let your foot slip: He will not doze, your guardian.

Behold, He will not doze or sleep, the guardian of Israel. The Lord is your guardian, the Lord is your shade; He is at your right hand. By day the sun will not strike you; nor the moon by night. The Lord will guard you from all harm; the Lord will guard your life. The Lord will guard your coming and your going both now and for ever.

† *Glory be to the Father and to the Son and to the Holy Spirit, as it was in the beginning, is now, and ever shall be, world without end. Amen. Alleluia.*

The Lord will guard you from every evil. May the Lord guard your soul.

Psalm 129 (130)

Out of the depths

If You took notice of our wickedness, Lord—Lord, who, would survive? Out of the depths I have cried to You, Lord: Lord, hear my voice. Let Your ears listen out for the voice of my pleading. If You took notice of our transgressions, Lord—Lord, who would be left? But with You is forgiveness, and for this we revere You.

I rely on You, Lord, my spirit relies on Your promise; my soul hopes in the Lord, more than the watchman for daybreak. More than the watchman for daybreak, let Israel hope in the Lord: for with the Lord there is kindness and abundant redemption. He himself will redeem Israel from all its transgressions.

† *Glory be to the Father and to the Son and to the Holy Spirit, as it was in the beginning, is now, and ever shall be, world without end. Amen. Alleluia.*

If you took notice of our wickedness, Lord—Lord, who, would survive?

Canticle: Philippians 2

Christl, God's servant

Just as the Father raises the dead and gives them life, so the Son, too, gives life to whom He will.

Jesus Christ, although He shared God's nature, did not try to seize equality with God for Himself; but emptied Himself, took on the form of a slave, and became like a man: not in appearance only, for He humbled himself by accepting death, even death on a cross.

For this, God has raised Him high, and given Him the name that is above every name, so that at the name of Jesus every knee will bend, in Heaven, on earth, and under the earth, and every tongue will proclaim

"Jesus Christ is Lord," to the glory of God the Father.

✝ *Glory be to the Father and to the Son and to the Holy Spirit, as it was in the beginning, is now, and ever shall be, world without end. Amen. Alleluia.*

Just as the Father raises the dead and gives them life, so the Son, too, gives life to whom He will.

Short reading: 1 Corinthians 15:55–57

Death, where is your victory? Death, where is your sting? Now the sting of death is sin, and sin gets its power from the Law. So let us thank God for giving us the victory through our Lord Jesus Christ.

Canticle: Magnificat

My soul rejoices in the Lord

All that the Father has given into My care will come to Me. Whoever comes to Me, I will not throw him out.

My soul proclaims the greatness of the Lord, and my spirit rejoices in God, my salvation. For He has·shown me such favor—me, His lowly handmaiden. Now all generations will call me blessed, because the Mighty One has done great things for me.

His name is holy, His mercy lasts for generation after generation for those who revere Him. He has put forth His strength: He has scattered the proud and conceited, torn princes from their thrones; but lifted up the lowly. He has filled the hungry with good things; the rich He has sent away empty. He has come to the help of His servant Israel, He has remembered His mercy as He promised to our fathers, to Abraham and his children for ever.

† *Glory be to the Father and to the Son and to the Holy Spirit, as it was in the beginning, is now, and ever shall be, world without end. Amen. Alleluia.*

All that the Father has given into my care will come to me. Whoever comes to me, I will not throw him out.

Prayers and Intercession

Christ the Lord gives us the hope that our lowly bodies will take on the form of His body of light. And so let us acclaim Him:
Lord, You are our life and our resurrection.

Christ, Son of the living God, You raised Your friend Lazarus from the dead: raise the dead to life and glory, for You have redeemed them by Your precious blood.

Lord, You are our life and our resurrection.

Christ, consoler of those who mourn, You wiped away the tears of Lazarus' family, of Jairus and the widow of Naim: bring consolation and comfort to all who mourn their dead.

Lord, You are our life and our resurrection.

Christ, our Savior, dethrone sin from ruling over our mortal bodies, so that just as we have deserved death as the wages of sin, we may receive the reward of eternal life in You.

Lord, You are our life and our resurrection.

Christ, our redeemer, look upon those who have no hope because they do not know You: make them believe in the resurrection and the life of the world to come.

Lord, You are our life and our resurrection.

You gave the blind man the gift of seeing light, and abundant sight of You: show Your face to the dead who have not so far seen Your light.
Lord, You are our life and our resurrection.

At length You will permit our earthly home itself to disappear: grant us an eternal home in Heaven, one not made by human hands.
Lord, You are our life and our resurrection.

Our Father, Who art in Heaven, hallowed be Thy name. Thy kingdom come, Thy will be done on earth as it is in Heaven. Give us this day our daily bread, and forgive us our trespasses as we forgive those who trespass against us, and lead us not into temptation, but deliver us from evil.

Lord, in Your kindness accept our prayers: as our faith looks up to Your Son, risen from the dead, so may we receive a more solid hope of the future resurrection of Your servants. Through our Lord Jesus Christ, Your Son, Who lives and reigns with You in the unity of the Holy Spirit, God for ever and ever. Amen.

May the Lord bless us and keep us from all harm; and may He lead us to eternal life. Amen.

NOTES

Chapter 6

1. The Eucharistic Fast is the custom of refraining from food (but not liquids and medicines) for one hour prior to the Mass. This is meant to place oneself in the proper and prayerful frame of mind to receive the Eucharist.
2. Catechism of the Catholic Church Canon §1250–1253.
3. Jim Van Furst, "Jesus on Fasting an Penance," AmericanCath olic.org, February 11, 2009.

Chapter 7

1. This is a library of online sources concerning almsgiving. Gregory of Nyssa Home Page, http://www.sage.edu/faculty/salomd/nyssa/nfrnyssa.html.

Chapter 12

1. St. Catherine of Genoa, *Purgation and Purgatory: The Spiritual Dialogue* (Paulist Press, 1979).
2. Benedicta Ward, trans., *The Sayings of the Desert Fathers: The Alphabetical Collection* (Cistercian Publications, 1975), 103.

Chapter 15

1. In the case where a non-Catholic has requested burial in a Catholic cemetery, he can so interred as long as the person has been respectful of the Church during his lifetime and/or has shown some repentance for a previous lack of respect and no public scandal to the faithful would ensue (Can. 1184).

FURTHER READING

On God's Will for Our Lives

Gallagher, Timothy M., OMV
Discerning the Will of God: An Ignatian Guide to Christian Decision Making
Drawing from the timeless methods of Saint Ignatius of Loyola, this thought-ful meditation is enriched with examples and stories that offer practical and profound wisdom for aligning personal desires and goals with God's will. 978-0-8245-2489-0

On Death and Burial

Nouwen, Henri J. M.
Beyond the Mirror: Reflections on Death and Dying
With searing honesty Nouwen describes the events leading up to his near fatal accident and recalls the transformative experience at the portal of death. His insight inspires us to live our lives freely with confidence and trust that we belong to God. 978-0-8245-1961-2

D'Arcy, Paula
When People Grieve: The Power of Love in the Midst of Pain
This book is a compassionate road map for the bereaved and guides us with a deep understanding of what people need as they move through loss. 978-0-8245-2339-8

Aridas, Rev. Chris
The Catholic Funeral: The Church's Ministry of Hope
This comprehensive reference is an essential handbook for planning the end-of-life arrangements for a loved one. 978-0-8245-1750-2

On the Saints

Ellsberg, Robert
All Saints
This praised best-selling daily reader presents short, comprehensive biogra-phies of 365 saints and spiritual masters from Christianity and other faith traditions, including Mary Magdalene, Therese of Lisieux, Thomas Aqui-nas, Mother Teresa, Moses, Martin Luther King, Jr., and Gandhi. 978-0-8245-1679-6

Ellsberg, Robert
Blessed among All Women: Women Saints, Prophets, and Witnesses for Our Time
From Joan of Arc to Anne Frank and Mary Magdalene, Ellsberg offers insights into the way that women of all faiths and backgrounds have lived

out the lives of sanctity, mysticism, social justice, and world reform. 978-0-8245-2439-5

Compton, Madonna Sophia, Maria Compton Hernandez,
and Patricia Campbell
Women Saints: 365 Daily Readings
This charming book offers brief life stories, passionate readings, and uplifting prayers for daily inspiration about traditionally acknowledged saints alongside noble women of other religions, and heroines of the Old Testament. 978-0-8245-2413-5

On Prayer and Devotion

Keating, Thomas
Heart of the World
A clear, prophetic, and simple introduction to the contemplative tradition of Christianity and the ways open to Christians and non-Christians to enter the stream of this rich heritage of wisdom, literature, and meditative practice. 978-0-8245-2495-1

Keating, Thomas
Intimacy with God
Prominent Trappist monk and founder of the centering prayer movement Thomas Keating provides this poetic and accessible introduction to the method of Centering Prayer. 978-0-8245-2529-3

Nouwen, Henri J. M.
The Only Necessary Thing
Drawn from Nouwen's writings, this compilation of his thoughts, feelings, and struggles with prayer reveals the core of the man and his belief that prayer is the only necessary thing. 978-0-8245-2493-7

On the Mass

Champlain, Joseph M
Mystery and Meaning of the Mass
This acclaimed primer offers simple explanations about everything in the Catholic mass. 978-0-8245-2296-4

On the Mysteries

Caldecott, Stratford
The Seven Sacraments: Entering the Mystery of God
Stratford Caldecott is the former Director of the Chesterton Institute for Faith & Culture in Oxford, England. In this bold new elegant invitation to enter into the mysteries of the Christian faith he explains to Catholics and non-Catholics alike the mystical heart of the Catholic faith: the Seven Sacraments. 978-0-8245-2376-3

On the Church

Stagnaro, Angelo
The Catechist's Magic Kit: 80 Simple Tricks for Teaching Catholicism to Kids
The first and only Catholic book on Gospel Magic presents 80 tricks with easy to learn step-by-step illustrations. Approved for catechesis with the imprimatur. 978-0-8245-2518-7

Finley, Mitch
The Joy of Being Catholic
Celebrating the best of Catholic faith and culture, this affirmative gift book provides brief overviews of such topics as the sacraments, the scriptures, the saints, the arts, sex, and intellectual life. 978-0-8245-2572-9

On the Bible

Witherup, Ronald
The Bible Companion: A Catholic Handbook for Beginners
A prominent biblical scholar offers an entry-level overview of the Bible that presupposes no specialized knowledge of the Bible or of religion. 978-0-8245-1746-5

On the Love of God

Nouwen, Henri J. M.
Life of the Beloved: Spiritual Living in a Secular World
Initially written for a Jewish friend, this sincere testimony of the power and invitation of Christ has become Henri Nouwen's greatest legacy to Christians around the world. 978-0-8245-1986-5

ABOUT THE BOOK AND AUTHOR

Angelo Stagnaro, who has taught the Rite of Christian Initiation of Adults (RCIA) in Indiana and New York, has been a mentalist and magician since the age of thirteen and performs as the magician "Erasmus" on stage, television, and street corners in over a dozen countries, including Asia, Africa, and Europe. His books on magic, including *Conspiracy: A Guide to Mentalist Codes*, are bestsellers in several languages. In *The Christian Book of the Dead*, the author offers a Christian alternative to books such as *The Tibetan Book of the Dead* and *The Egyptian Book of the Dead*. Christians believe that the glory of being in God's presence in the afterlife is beyond our greatest imaginings and speculation. When, therefore, we reflect on the prospect of our inevitable death, we focus our gaze on this fleeting life: our connection to other people, who all undergo the same journey; our connection to God as our Source of Life Itself.